INHALE

INHALE

THE FRESH MEADOWS OF A GODLY PERSPECTIVE

GWENDOLYN ALEXANDER

ARPress
ILLUMINATING IDEAS,
EMPOWERING VOICES

Scripture is taken from the King James Version of the Bible.

Books by author, Gwendolyn Alexander, may be ordered eBook or soft cover by contacting:
Amazon.com, CreateSpace.com, and other online and retail outlets;
Amazon: **866-216-1072**

For special events, book signings, teaching sessions, speaking engagements, or ministry invitations, please contact directly:
Gwendolyn Alexander
amewoss@yahoo.com

Any people depicted in any imagery are models; and such imagery is used for informational purposes, only.

First self-published through CrossBooks, 2014
Republished through Westbow Press, 2016
Republished as a two-part series (It's Poetry! and It's Revelational!), 1/1/2018
Republished through Author Reputation Press, 2019

ARPress
45 Dan Road Suite 36
Canton MA 02021

Hotline: 1(800) 220-7660
Fax: 1(855) 752-6001

Ordering Information:
Quantity sales. Special discounts are available on quantity purchases by corporations, associations, and others. For details, contact the publisher at the address above.

Printed in the United States of America.

ISBN-13:   Paperback   978-8-89389-389-2
           eBook   979-8-89389-390-8

Library of Congress Control Number: 2024919043

And the Lord God formed man of the dust of the ground, and breathed into his nostrils the breath of life; and man became a living soul.

Genesis 2:7

Seeing He giveth to all life, and breath, and all things ...For in Him we live, and move, and have our being;

Acts 17:25b, 28a

Defined by: God
Born of: The Heart of Jesus Christ
Conceived of: The Holy Spirit
Written by: Gwendolyn Aileen Alexander

For my girls...

Girls, I pray for you a strong and determined strength of character to do God's will, that every Godly Truth you hear and read roots deeply in your heart. So that, like the cedars of Lebanon, you spring up in the power, might, and authority God has purposed for your life.

For your sakes, I sanctify myself.

LaQuita, my other first child,

I so enjoyed the times I spent with you and Audriana during your early years and shall forever cherish that close relationship. If I were allowed but one thing to impart to you this instance, it would be - What is impossible with man is possible with God. There is nothing too hard for God. No matter what the situation, God is poised to deliver. All you need do is let Him.

Audriana, my Precious,

My first niece, I vividly recall your early years, loving you like a daughter, and now I still adore you. Elder grandchild, big cousin, oldest sibling, like it or not, there is a God-given expectation and responsibility that comes with being the first. Your charge is to lead the way for the rest. I so praise God for covering and keeping you during the void of opportunity for me to continue nourishing you. I am thankful for renewed opportunities to share God with you. He is, as He has always been, setting things in order. Be encouraged that He does, indeed, favor you. Keep praying and keep trusting Him. He has awesome things in store.

Jai-Jai, Superstar,

My dear godchild, sometimes I have to scratch my head and question, "Is this true?" I feel so absentee in that role. Well, dear, you've grown into a lovely young lady and I'm proud of you. You are at a place many girls, even women, struggle all their lives to find—contentment. You content yourself with being right where you are, not rushing a thing. Simply okay with you in the midst of a world that is so different whether someone or no one at all is there to share it.

If I had one thing to impart to you, it would be - Seriously consider Jesus, Dear Heart. It is in Him only that these good things can be sustained. For without Him, anything that you accomplish is merely accomplished in vanity—with no power to change lives now or to live on after we are gone.

You are an avid reader like your mother, a quest God has given you. God wants me to give you this input regarding it - with all your getting, get understanding. There is no real understanding apart from the Word of God which is Jesus Christ. Remember, He gives the free gift of the Holy Spirit who imparts to us the revelations of understanding. Without Him, it's only knowledge without power; and God wants to do powerful things through us. You are soon to be off to college and somewhat on your own. My fervent prayer is that you go through it in 'Righteous' company.

Yendami, My Girl,
You inspire me, my darling. I so thank God for you, your place in my heart and your place on this earth, as defined by Him. Though others may have missed it, I see a girl who is comfortable in her own skin and unfazed by the opinions, views, and standards of the world around her. God has given you a place of innocence. Stay there for as long as He'll allow you; and soak Him up at every chance.

My Precious **Gnywe**,
You are my oldest, a precious gift from God. I'm so grateful he gave me you. Ma' Sweets, you came and brought true sweetness to my life. I remember vividly what God spoke to me the February before you were born. It was in the 7th year of my marriage that you were to be born. It hadn't crossed my mind in this capacity until God said it. He spoke to me by His Sweet Spirit, "You know 7 is my number." I tell you, God perfected a work in my body to bring you into this world and my prayer is that He continues to perfect you as you grow in grace. May you, even in your youth, walk close to and enjoy intimacy with your God.

Your God-mother (T-Jackie) scrambled the letters of my name and out of it came yours. An extension of Gwendolyn, you are. However, my prayer and desire for you is that you walk out my God's Truth and live His Righteousness 'better' than me; trust and follow Him completely; and allow the wisdom that I have gained because of my mistakes guide you such that mine not be yours.

My Big Girl, you are, as God spoke it, 'strength'. Just 12 and wearing a woman's size 12 shoe. Be not discouraged or dismayed, for God has spoken that He made you with 'advantage'. Walk in it. A power-house in Jesus, may you stand tearing down the kingdom of the enemy while building up the walls of the Kingdom of our God.

Ariana, congenial, bubbly you; a jewel in the crown of the Master. May you always be as bright and cheerful; and may the light of Christ in you shine as brilliant. The girls and I are always so refreshed by your warm embrace. You are family, indeed, given by God, forever. May your great people skills be always useful to the glory of God that He may, through you, draw many to righteousness.

My Sweetie Peati, **Neziah**, My Baby, My Shadow, 'Nizzi-you-make-me-dizzy',

I tried to make you a daddy's baby, but you wouldn't hear of it. Here I am 10 years later with you still under me, attached at the hip. I can't breathe without you trying to share my air. Still, ten years later, I am loving it. Your devotion and unconditional love is my sunshine. It amazes me that you still love Mommy today as strong as ever. So intense, it is my prayer and covenant with God that He not allow your incredible love and devotion to be lost by me to any mortal man but that He would transfer it to Himself. As you grow in grace, may your dedication to Him be as intense and driven. May you learn to curl up in His lap, talk His ear off, and call on Him to watch all your new tricks, to listen to you sing, to help you design your many project ideas, to encourage you, to protect you, to impart wisdom and strength.

You add sweetness to my veggies, My Sweet Pea (smile)! Of the many things I love about you, I have to say that I like best the meaning of your name, "pure victory", as you concluded from the many internet searches we did. May you always triumph in the riches of God's glory in you. Not only do you look just like Mommy, but your personality and character reflect so strongly mine; my prayer and desire is for God's strength and direction to reinforce in you the 'God' parts and to impart unto you wisdom to steer clear of the bad parts.

'Boldness' God has spoken of you. May God mold and strengthen you to grow in that boldness for the Kingdom's sake; to go and speak Truth's others dare not - preaching in season and out - with the Holy Spirit, your confidence.

Shekinah, Keedi, Shaq,
I remember when your momma and I found out that we were pregnant at the same time. God spoke to my Spirit that February, "Lagniappe". Something extra special, above and beyond the standard, was in store. Then came the term, God called it and it was so. You and Neziah were born within 18 minutes of each other - Twin Cousins! The unfolding of this event was so much more than you could ever imagine and I'm so excited to watch the continuation of the story.

My sharp, quick-wit niece, you are. I know you don't like it sometimes, but 'T' is here to help you keep it in perspective so that God's purpose in it is not quenched. I have to tell you, I was so excited when you called to let me know you had made the awesome decision to accept Jesus and be baptized (September 2011). The angels in Heaven rejoiced over you and I joined the celebration.

When I think on experiences that make me proud, you show up in those thoughts. I'm looking forward to the memories to come. May the Shekinah glory of God be imbedded in the deep reaches of your person and always pierce through to reveal His Truth and to light up the world around you.

Zneyah, T-Baby, Z-Boo,

I love you! You know you are my girl, and I just love hanging out with you. Though you are certifiable, it's true; I wouldn't trade you for the world. There is a wrestle inside of you that I know there's the power of God to prevail. The Spirit of God is your helper. Remember the things that I have told you; when you are ready, let Jesus in and it will all be settled. In the meantime and beyond, **in the power of Jesus' name, I speak peace over you, my sweet angel**.

Colorful you are. The beautiful colors of the rainbow are you.

Alex, Girlie,

Bright-eyed, bushy tailed with a beautiful smile, I can't help but smile back at. You've got personality, T-Baby; may God design it and define it all His own. I pray for you the blessings of health, strength and clarity. May you be clear on what is right versus what is wrong and always choose right. May God protect and guard your heart and mind; and may you always shine as bright in your heart as your outward smile. I love you!

Z'Hara, My Girl,

You're going to scorn me for this one, but I tell you, the word that came to my spirit when I thought on you and what to write was "fireball". You see, a fireball has the ability to travel through and light on, and light up, not only what it touches but the environment around it. Be careful to ensure that each morning and opportunity during the day, it's lit and re-lit by the fire of the Holy Ghost. God is poised to do some awesome wonders through your ministry and those amazing musical talents He has graced you with. My prayer is that everything God has purposed for your life especially your Christian witness, be met. May every standing opposition (even that in you) be removed and the fullness of God's purpose be released.

Arie'L, Dear Heart,

I so miss hanging out with you. We've got to get together soon, Girlie. I'm so glad God allowed me the opportunities that I've had. There are not many young people with such an impressive connection with and desire for God, as you. Hold on tight and may that fire ever burn in you. I know you'll do well. It's inevitable for the God in you can't lose.

For the Guys…3Way, Charlie, and Nigel (*and my great-nephews, little Audrick and Mason*), and **Aaron Levy**

Well guys, what can I say that I haven't already said? First, let me share a little knowledge with you. God has set the order of things both spiritual and physical. In the natural, earthly realm, He has given the male charge to lead. The man is to lead "keeping God's Word". The world will tell you that you should do the things that boys do while they are young; you should have fun, live free, and get it out of your system; you should freely sew your 'wild' oats before you marry. 'T' is compelled to declare to you that this is a lie from the pits of hell. God's Word says to flee from these things and to touch not that which is unclean. The world has perpetrated that this primarily applies to the female, when God actually established the order of things to be in the hands of the male. You are the head in the keeping of His Word. His Law is first charged to you. He has established that by your leadership the female will also line up with His will.

Paul implored Timothy, "*Let no man despise thy youth; but be thou an example of the believer, in word, in conversation, in charity [love], in spirit, in faith, in purity.*" (I Timothy 4:12) Know that God called many young men and boys throughout the Bible to be separated, set apart, and to lead the way—Samuel, David, Solomon, Jeremiah, Hananiah, Mishael, Azariah, Timothy and more. He gave them the ability to accomplish their charge because in their hearts they desired to do His will. He is able to do the same for you if you invite Him to do so.

My prayer for each of you is that you realize as a male the charge of righteousness is to you first. Let your living be like that of Daniel and the three Hebrew boys—purpose in your hearts not to sin against your God. My greatest hope for you is that you fulfill your calling, secure the standard, and walk in Jesus' excellence.

Giving Honor To:

God – The maker, creator, and sustainer of this universe and the Father of us all.

Jesus – The living, walking, breathing Word of God; The means by which God dwelled among us and became in touch with our infirmities. As my friend, He shed blood that will never lose its power and became my Savior.

Holy Spirit – The means by which God takes up His abode in us, quickens us, and inspires us. He who comforts, leads, guides, and directs my living.

CONTENTS

iNHALE
FOREWORD

Inhalation is a process of breathing called inspiration. Oxygen is pulled in through the mouth or nose to be distributed throughout the body as required to sustain life. This distribution of Oxygen incites chemical activity within the body and releases energy. It not only releases energy within the body, but also causes a release of Carbon Dioxide which is required to sustain plant life. This energy within the body also drives a release of waste (the useless stuff) to sustain, promote, and fortify the health of the same.

From the respiratory center, bursts of impulses signal the muscles that drive inhalation. According to the body's need these muscles are driven to speed up or slowdown the rate of intake.

We can only feel air, but it is as real as anything we can see or physically touch. Air is vital to sustaining life. People have been known to live for extended periods without water (7 days) and without food (30 days); but without air, without Oxygen, life expires within minutes.

The value of air even goes beyond simply sustaining life through respiration, but shields the earth's atmosphere from harmful sun rays, and even traps heat from it. It also protects us from objects in space, including meteors.

Clearly, the air of our intake is of exceptional importance to our very existence.

In Christendom, the air [the Word] of our intake is more valuable than can be fully expressed, for its importance drives both our physical and spiritual existence. The intake of God's Word is the breath of spiritual life that fuels our living. By it, we take in Jesus. We therefore take in a living entity. By God's provision, He enters the heart of man and is distributed by the Spirit to empower and drive God's righteousness in us.

As we take in Jesus, the Word of God, and grow in grace, may the things that are out of order grow more undesirable to us. In time, may these undesirables be purged, detached, eliminated from our intake. In the 'Word' of our intake, the Holy Spirit is our respiratory center. He drives it, quickens it in us, and by the power of God causes its every value to be released in us. He is the means by which all things become new and the old (undesirables - impure, contaminated, sinful stuff) is passed away and purged from us. By this same intake, He energizes, empowers us to accomplish every assignment.

When I think of my inhale, I can't help but think of the smells that sometimes come with the breathing. Some breaths come with rotten, repugnant odors, which may leave us greatly affected and, in some cases, physically ill. Oh, how pleasant it is to take in air that is accompanied by a pleasant order. The more deeply we breathe. So great is its effect on our physical and our psyche, we have worked to duplicate these smells—flowers, spices, fruits—even through artificial means. We purchase air fresheners, incense, candles, aerosols sprays, powders, soaps, perfumes, colognes, the list goes on. These items run out and we go buy more. With great effort we are driven, trying to maintain the temporal.

In truth, fragrance plays a significant role in the quality of our air intake. The better, more pleasant and desirable the smell, the greater the inhale! Let Jesus be our inhale—a good, strong, powerful, lasting incense. With the sweetest breezes, He enters to fill every crook, crevice, nook, and cranny to remove all things unpleasant. He is the sweet savor, the magnificent flavor of Truth. When taken in, He in all sufficiency supplies our most vital parts—mind, body, and spirit.

The writings in this book are designed and given by God to reflect the many facets of that inhale—what we take in, what it is designed to accomplish and to fortify in us, and what should come out of us as a result of its life-sustaining provision. May you soak up Jesus with every page.

My prayerful desire is to inspire, edify, encourage, convict, instruct you, and relate to you. Above all, I desire to drive you, to pull you into a greater depth of desire for my Jesus that you inhale deeply and in all that you get, get God;

For the end of the matter is this:
Let us hear the conclusion of the whole matter:
Fear God, and keep His commandments:
for this is the whole duty of man.

Ecclesiastes 12:13

PART 1

THE FRESH MEADOWS OF A GODLY PERSPECTIVE– IT'S POETRY!

See the foreword for an explanation of the
first part of this book's compilations.

I

YOU ARE THE AIR
THAT I BREATHE

In the meadow, in the beauty of
Your Holiness, are the 'sweetest' views

*Guide my hands, Dear Lord, and let me paint a picture for
the world to see Your beauty I experience within me.*

NOTHING COMPARES!

Oh, I remember well God's precious gift of words for me to amazingly express Him. God initiated this Psalm several years ago during a study of Job Chapters 38-41. To Job, God spoke of Himself in chapters 38-41 with profound words.

An especially awe-inspiring precept for me was God's exclamation in honoring Moses' request to show him His Glory (Exodus 33:18-23. *And the LORD descended in the cloud, and stood with him there, and proclaimed the name of the LORD. And the LORD passed by before him, and proclaimed, The LORD, The LORD God, merciful and gracious, longsuffering, and abundant in goodness and truth, Keeping mercy for thousands, forgiving iniquity and transgression and sin, and that will by no means clear the guilty; visiting the iniquity of the fathers upon the children, and upon the children's children, unto the third and to the fourth generation. Exodus 34:5-7*

The study of David, part of a 2008 Lifeway bible study series, jarred my memory triggering me to reflect. I Chronicles chapter 29, particularly verses 10 through 15, brought a refreshing. The beauty of the words spoken in those verses by David re-birthed in me and I begin to scribe the words spoken to my heart by God four years prior.

The Psalm that God drew out of my heart and put to words follows. May it bless and excite you about the excellence of your adoption, fellow Sons of God.

What an awesome God is our Father!

NOTHING COMPARES!
To You, My King!

If I had ten thousand tongues, I could not praise Him enough
For there are no words which sufficiently ascribe my God!
He is the culmination of all that IS, WAS, and ever hopes TO BE.
He is a treasure more precious than rubies, more precious than the rarest gems.

No mountain extends high enough to reach the heights of Him.
No valley flows low enough to reach the depths of Him.
No measure can reflect the vastness of Him.
For the length of my God has no end.

His volume knows no boundaries.
Time does not limit Him; does not deplete Him nor assign Him years.
For, before time was, He IS!
He is the Ancient of Days, the Father of Time.

No logic can make sense of Him;
At the Master's presence, our logic is rendered helpless.
Our mind cannot conceive the extent of Him.
Our heart cannot contain the fullness of Him.

His Beauty is beyond description.
His Glory outshines the sun.
His Holiness is purer than water, purer than refined gold.
His Righteousness defines all and settles EVERY matter.

Every bit of energy this universe holds, His power exceeds it!
There is no might that can exceed His; no authority that can override Him.
There is no weapon mightier, none more capable, none sharper than His Word…

Yet, His LOVE, His GRACE, His MERCY out-measure them all!

GOD IS

Periodically, by assignment, I led the lesson review and discussion for the Baptist Training Union (BTU) class at Mt. Airy. Having long taken the position to never turn God down, without question, one particular Sunday, I responded 'yes' to an assignment with no concern for the subject matter. When God directs someone's heart to use me in sharing His Word, I accept.

Opening the BTU book days later to prepare for my assignment, I realized the subject of the lesson was 'Who is God?' Reflectively, it took me back to learning to write book reports in middle school. Students were encouraged to pick a subject of interest then narrow it to a more focused, less broad, subject. That generally took several iterations as narrower and narrower subjects were identified until an easier, more manageable final subject was realized.

Who is God? Certainly, there is nothing whatsoever narrow or condensed about this subject. I chuckled to the Master, "Okay Lord. No human being has the capacity to answer this one. You are huge—the largest possible subject in existence. So, You have to feed me and give me a means to express this one in a manner digestible by the limited mental and intellectual capacity of man."

Seeking out this matter by recording the Jehovah characters of God, I began writing down all that I knew then researching to find more. Further, scripture that supported each character was identified. The result of this effort was much to take in. However, it didn't settle the burning I had that it must come to a concise and mentally digestible point.

God reminded me of Moses who inquired similarly. Who do I tell them has sent me? Who do I tell them You are? God responded, "Tell them I AM has sent you. I AM that I AM." Continuing to ponder, as usual I questioned God, "Exactly what does that mean?" Realizing that only He could answer the question and present this lesson, I took a position like Moses for Him to tell me what to say to His people. He faithfully and justly responded. What He had to say was profound. Only God can define God. This is what He had to say of Himself

GOD IS
(September 2004)

God IS!!!
Put simply, "He IS!"

He is the fullness, the completeness of EXISTENCE.
He is THEE by which all things exist.
God is the Maker, Creator, and the Sustainer of the universe.
He is the culmination of all that IS, WAS, and SHALL YET BE.

Besides Him there is none other.
None can define Him, except Him.

Everything that He speaks is He.
He is everything that He does.
What He says and does defines Him;
For, God is what He says and God is what He does.

"God is Who?"
God is that which defines God.

His Spirit said to my spirit:
"He is the Great I AM THAT I AM."
God responded, "What do you need My Child?"
Then, 'THAT' I AM!

It is not a question to ponder; to be searched out; or written down;
For to 'know' Who God is, is to 'experience' God, to try Him for
yourself.

You see...
If you need a lawyer, He'll meet you in the courtroom.
If you need a doctor, He is your healer.
If you need a miracle, He is a way out of no-way.
If you need support, He is your heavy load sharer.

If you need mercy, He is your salvation.

If you need someone to talk to, He is Wonderful Counselor.

If you need a mother, He'll rock you to sleep at night.

If you need a father, He'll care for and protect you.

If you need deliverance, He knows your thoughts afar off and will answer before you call.

If you need understanding, He is master teacher and He will impart unto you divine knowledge.

If you need peace, He is your bridge over troubled waters.

If you need relief, He is your calm in the midst of a storm.

If you need direction or guidance, He is a compass for your way.

If you need a breakthrough, He is your wheel in the middle of a wheel.

If you need a job, He will make the assignment.

If you need a refreshing, He'll mold and reshape you; He'll even change your name.

GOD is EVERYTHING!

He is everything good, and everything good is He!

He is ALL THINGS at ALL TIMES.

He is whatever you need, when you need it.

PERMANENT INK

A co-worker expressed an issue with the missing 'o' in my email correspondences—"God morning" instead of "Good morning"—citing it as a mistake that I needed to correct. I responded to the effect "No mistake; just a blessing". The individual expressed discontentment with my use of such words. The exchange exposed the individual's lack of belief in God. Interestingly, shortly thereafter, HR relayed another complaint from a different individual, I assumed.

Smiling, I talked with God. "Well, Lord, I suspected this would come to an end eventually. It did the heart good while it lasted. Know that God had given me the revelation of that greeting years ago when at my first place of employment. I used it continuously until this written notice of rejection at the third major company. Though 2 rejected the greeting, great were the accolades from those who were blessed by it. For that, I am grateful. So, as not to offend the minority, the greeting has been discontinued.

After the first rejection, these words pervaded my thoughts. Be encouraged against the odds, my brethren, for **God is a permanent force that no mortal man by rejection can cause to cease from existence**.

News of the second rejection caused me to ponder, "Father, how do I go back to 'good' after the revelation you gave me to drop the 'o'?" Not feeling it, I resolved to include in my greeting only "hello" and/or the recipient's name. "Good morning/afternoon" seemed insufficient for the blessing imparted through "God morning."

God gently spoke to my spirit, *"There is none good but God. No matter how it looks or sounds, all day long 'Good' is one and the same as 'God' with an extra 'o'."*

Yeah, they look different, even sound different, but Truth says: "They are one and the same!"

See Mark 10:18; James 1:17

PERMANENT INK
(Inerasable, June 2013)

Our God is not finite, ambiguous, nor indistinct...
He is a revelational God
He cannot be contained in a book
Nor can the reality of Him be confined by the mind of man.

He is an experience;
He is a presence;
He is a feeling.

The Truth of His existence is locked tight, tamper-proof and impenetrable.
His Word, grounded and never to be uprooted;
His Word is not conventional—
It does not begin and end with the letters on a page.
It is not restricted, nor confined.
It is a living, breathing entity that reveals itself in new, different, refined,
and more mature ways each time a pure heart reads, hears, or meditates on it.

Without apprehension, My God's precepts are solid and sure.
His love is firmly fixed and unwavering.
His righteousness, established and unshakable.

He is Peace!
He is Joy beyond articulation!
He is Truth!
He is Life!

My God cannot be restricted by our limited carnal/physical views.
He cannot be restrained by our unwillingness to accept Him,
Nor decreased by our inability to make sense of Him.

He is not a man;
He is not flesh;
He is not made with hands.

He supersedes the physical.
He is existence—the unshakable force that holds all things, even the physical, together.
He is that which, though denounced, cannot be revoked!
He is a resolute, immovable, rock solid source!

He is the Intangible!
He is the Word!
He is the Authority!
He is the Majority!

His sovereignty cannot be revoked by man's desire to cancel Him.
His name is not erasable by man's determination to blot Him out.
His authority is not commutable by man's attempt to legislate Him.

He is Power!
He is Glory!
He is Grace!
He is Mercy!

His deity is valid and in force, a solid endorsement.
His authority cannot be commuted.
His power is absolute and immutable.
His Truth is settled and secure,

Without apology, **in permanent ink**, He stands the Creator, the Godhead, the establisher of the law and the executor of judgment.

GOOD MORNING FATHER

For many, it is a struggle getting through one day to another. The enemy takes advantage, especially in times of drought such as economic difficulties, work challenges, and relationship challenges. He attempts to dangle before us his artificial relief or even entices us with worries designed to keep us bogged down and ineffective.

But, we have an adversary and an anchor that we can look to stand in the gap, to fight for us and even be the strength we need to hold us up. Even if we find ourselves slipping in the midst of the weights that challenge us, we take confidence that He understands and is faithful to recover us. Be confident in each day that God is the author of it and in authority over it.

Prevalent among the Psalms on my heart when writing this prayer was Psalm 118 and particularly verse 24.

GOOD MORNING FATHER
(4th Quarter, 2007)

You've been so good and I thank You.

Thank You, Lord God, for sweet rest in the assurance of Your Word
That You neither slumber nor do You sleep,
That the sun may not smite us by day or the moon by night,
That we wake to new dew every morning upon the ground
As fresh and new are Your Grace and Your Tender Mercies
Which cover us in all-sufficient supply.

To know You is to adore You, Oh Magnificent God.
"Hallelujah and Glory!"
We shout as we look with anticipation unto the day ahead
Knowing that our covering and our strength is ever before us.
And in the company of Your Holy Spirit, we take confidence.
We take refuge this day in Your Word—the order of our steps.

We raise our eyelids in vivid awareness
That our adversary is actively seeking to entrap us,
And stands as our constant accuser before the Father.
With confidence that our God has granted us
And our Savior has secured,
We can take authority over all the powers of the wicked one;

Where this flesh fails to line itself up completely,
We take further confidence in our companion, the Holy Spirit, who
intercedes for us,
And in our Savior who sits at the right hand of the Father.
Our High Priest and mediator
Showing forth His blood which has cleansed us from all unrighteousness
And granted us the right to be called 'Sons of God'.

This is a day that the Lord has made.
I rejoice; and I am glad!!!

UNBELIEVABLE
(A Christmas Sonnet, December 2013)

After Bible study one Wednesday evening, an aunt reminded me of our Christmas program on the upcoming Sunday immediately following Sunday School and that I should certainly have something prepared. That night, I pondered various writings of mine and was satisfied that none fit. Further, simply pulling from some cliché writing or reading a scripture never satisfies my heart regarding Jesus for it is my conviction that He deserves so much more from me - something personal.

As always, I petitioned my resource to extract a personal composition. After all, He put it in me, so who better to pull it out. Driving in to work Thursday morning, I spoke to God, "Father give the words from my heart to express what the miraculous birth of my Savior is all about." Immediately, speaking through the Holy Spirit, He reminded me of a writing that He had begun in me two months prior.

At that time, connecting with not much more than the title, I typed 'UNBELIEVABLE' and saved the otherwise empty document under the same name. In my meditations, I thought about it several times after, but no words came. I resolved that it was not time and simply spoke to the Holy Spirit, "I'm ready. Just don't let me miss the appointed reveal, so that I can finish it." Here it is pouring out months later, at the purposed time.

What God did in sending Jesus is indeed an exposition of awesome, incomprehensible love.

Yet, I believe!

UNBELIEVABLE
(A Christmas Sonnet, December 2013)
Who hath believed our report? and to whom is the arm of the Lord revealed?
Isaiah 53:1

Unbelievable,
That Son of Almighty God would dutifully become the son of weak man,
That a King would walk away from His riches untold and enter this place of poverty,
That Royalty would leave behind His royal robe to put on peasant clothes,
That the Glory of God would choose to enter this place of shame,
…just to sup with lowly me.
Unbelievable, yet I BELIEVE.

Unbelievable,
That Covering would come to need shelter,
That Providence would be exchanged for adversity,
That Light would so eagerly step into darkness,
That Order would deliberately establish His presence amidst chaos,
…just to enlighten sinful me.
Unbelievable, yet I BELIEVE.

Unbelievable,
That Infinite Word would take on finite existence,
That a Power House would step aside from His sovereignty to take company with the powerless,
That Omnipresence would submit to being confined in flesh,
That Omniscient Love without apprehension would desire to fellowship with the wicked and unreliable,
…just to embrace undesirable me.
Unbelievable, yet I BELIEVE.

Unbelievable,
That Incorruptible would take the form of corruptible,
That Spiritually Unrestrained would accept physical limitation,

That Author of Liberty would choose to be restrained,
That Purity would take on the appearance of impurity,
…just to relate to contemptible me.
Unbelievable, yet I BELIEVE.

Unbelievable,
That Overflowing Provision would shift to need
That Self-Sustained would willfully become dependent,
That Plenty would willingly turn to lack,
That Grace would deliberately come to suffer disgrace.
…just to bless unworthy me.
Unbelievable, yet I BELIEVE.

Unbelievable,
That Life would submit to death,
That Beginning would be commuted to end.
That the Top would choose the bottom,
That Above would shift to Below,
…just to exalt insignificant me.
Unbelievable, yet I BELIEVE.

Unbelievable,
That Unblemished Lamb would take on flawed flesh;
That Amazing God, Himself, would submit to the form and consequence
of ordinary Man,
That Perfect Friend would willingly enter the presence of enemies,
That Innocence would passively take on guilt,
…just to save a wretch like me
Unbelievable, yet I BELIEVE.

16

IMPOSSIBLE
(A Resurrection Day Sonnet, December 2013)

After adding 'Unbelievable' in mid-December, I was most certain of this book's completeness. There couldn't possibly be anything else. Amazingly, God gave me more.

During the Christmas program at New Covenant Christian Fellowship Church in Crystal Springs, MS, the pastor expounded on the value of Christmas and the coming Savior. Reflecting on Jesus' coming in the shape, form, and fashion of flesh, the pastor began an exposition of His ultimate purpose and eventual accomplishment by way of the cross. Hearing God say "Impossible", this Resurrection Day sonnet was born.

That God would end with this makes sense. **The end, the seal to all that Jesus did while on this earth was in the power of His resurrection**. A body that endured scourging and suffered death got up from the grave-an impossible feat. Access to deliverance and pardoning brought by one accursed is inconceivable by the human mind not the heart!

IMPOSSIBLE
(A Resurrection Day Sonnet, December 2013)

The things which are impossible with men are possible with God. Luke 18:27

Impossible,
That the tears of mourning could produce the Oil of Joy,
That trash could be transformed to Treasure,
That ashes would be the Origin of Beauty,
That imperfection can expose Perfection,
That in sorrow can be found Triumph,
… but to justify the guilty.
Impossible, yet Jesus did!

Impossible,
That to be broken is to cause to be Mended,
That be shattered is to make Whole,
That to be decreased could yield Increase,
That damnation would bring Salvation,
That the crushing blows of defeat were actually the noise of Victory,
…but to free the enslaved.
Impossible, yet Jesus did!

Impossible,
That becoming diseased would unleash the Power of Healing,
That out of a curse would ascend a Blessing,
That rejection would institute a foundation for Inclusion and Adoption,
That iniquity would be transmuted Righteousness,
That the spilling of blood could bestow a veil of Virtue,
…but to cleanse the filthy.
Impossible, yet Jesus did!

Impossible,
That separation could breed Reconciliation,
That forsaking a Son would grant rights of Inheritance to many sons,
That pain and agony could give birth to Purpose,

That the victim of riot would indict offerings of Peace,
That the sightless could be given Vision,
…but to bless the cursed.
Impossible, yet Jesus did!

Impossible,
That death would dispense Life,
That blame would remit Innocence,
That false witness could propagate Truth,
That condemnation would exact Justification,
That being mantled with sin would harvest Purification,
…but to bring life to murderers.
Impossible, yet Jesus did!

Impossible,
That the pains of despair would yield an offering of Hope,
That no would become Yes,
That flesh could commune with Spirit,
That the burden of disgrace could enact the gift of Grace,
That that which was finished convened the Beginning,
…but to marry the divorced.
Impossible, yet Jesus did!

Impossible,
That Heaven would visit hell,
That from death could commence Perpetual Life,
That from surrender would emerge the power of Deliverance,
That the disparaging chains of bondage could reach the pinnacle of Freedom,
That exaltation of power and authority would be sanctioned in a Name,
…but to share an inheritance with the outcast.
Impossible, yet Jesus did!

The power of Jesus' resurrection has unleashed a current and a coming victory that cannot be stopped.

IN JESUS, FREE

I sat in church service on Sunday morning, July 3rd, to a program of celebration of liberty, in honor of the upcoming 4th of July Independence Day celebration for our great nation. I had grabbed my bible for services as I usually do, but today felt compelled to also bring along a tablet for notes.

I remember well the text that was the basis of the sermon for the day: Galatians 5:13-15. Of course, as I listened through the sermon, my mind went back particularly to Galatians 5:1, *Stand fast, therefore, in the liberty wherewith Christ hath made us free, and be not entangled again with the yoke of bondage.* At that moment the Spirit began to minister to me regarding True Freedom and Christ being that freedom, that liberty, that we as Christians have been given rights and free access to.

I heard the entire sermon and even have things written down as spoken by the assistant pastor that morning; yet, in the process of that exchange, the Holy Spirit ministered to me, as well. He began to expound Jesus as my liberty in the most profound words; those expressions of freedom are written in this text.

May your heart be enlightened and strengthened knowing that there is a most beautiful way of escape from every temptation you find yourself in. May you be drawn to a place of liberty that further distances you from those temptations as you grow in grace.

Anointed, God appointed song writer, Tye Tribett puts it well:
Sin no longer has control of me.
I walk in liberty.
I'm free!!!

IN JESUS, FREE
(July 3, 2011)

Jesus is my standard, my statue of liberty.
He untangled the serpent's knot and He set me free.
He removed my chains of bondage and by His power, He released me.

He is the rock upon which stands my defense
In 'ultimate sacrifice'; He went down into darkness
With all power, He rose the 'ultimate authority'

In His name alone is my secure confidence.
He has broken, even removed the yoke of my burden,
By His yoke, He has lifted me.

He is the express Word of God
Which took on flesh, dwelt among man, taught man how to live;
He has become the 'order of my steps'.

He is Thee Monarch to whom I stand submissive, obedient
My faith is established and made complete in Him.

My ransom, man insufficient to fund,
He paid it with His life.
He became my Deliverer.

He suffered
Died in my stead;
He became my Savior.

He laid a firm foundation;
In the power of His name, He established me
He became my anchor.

To the prison of sin I was chained and set to be enslaved.
He shed blood that will never lose its power
He became my way of escape.

He is the innocent, upon whose shoulders all my crimes were placed;
Faultless, He pled guilty;
He, my case, dismissed.

Though completely right, He suffered the wrong and established me;
I am exempt from condemnation for He has become my Righteousness.

In filthiness, I stood before Him - wretched, insufficient, dung;
Yet, with great power He has redeemed me.
My insufficiencies, made sufficient in Him.

The enemy, my heels did bruise.
I fell, defeated it seemed but He has imparted his authority;
With Him I am the majority; I cannot be held down for He is my
champion.

Truth, in brilliant, pure light came down to earth;
Canceled the darkness; revealed the way;
No more to stumble, He has made my path straight.

He who was dead and now lives left this earth for His throne on High.
However, in the Spirit of His authority, returned to dwell in me and
set my course.
He's the compass for my way thus sin is no longer the rule in me.

He, from the beginning, is the Word that stands above the law;
I am no longer judged but justified.

In my stead
He hung there on that tree.
He delivered me;
He set me free,
He is **Jesus, My Liberty!**

SWEET SAVOR

A saturating fragrance is my Jesus—a lingering perfume of the most invigorating release. Thoughts of Him and all His benefits play on the mind the sweetest refrain.

I asked God for this piece to reflect names and attributes of my Jesus not commonly noted or expressed when speaking or writing of Him; ones that would affect a tension and attention in us that would press us, humble us, and even inspire us, hopefully the rest of our days.

My Jesus, he is the total of the characters of Yaweh and attributes of Almighty God caused to embody the likeness of flesh. He is

PURITY,

RIGHTEOUSNESS,

SINLESSNESS IN THE FLESH,

AMAZING GOD,

AMAZING KING!

Put simply, I just wanted to reflect what I breathe in when I inhale while thinking on the indescribable beauty and precious value of my Savior.

My hope is that you can or eventually come to relate and heartily agree.

SWEET SAVOR
Hallelujah, Sweet Jesus!

He that openeth and no man shutteth,
Has given us the keys to heaven,
Open access to the throne room of the Most High.

God's Word incarnate
The manifestation of God's Word in the form of flesh
The living, walking, breathing Word of God
He is further revelation of the awesome,
Untouchable mind of God.

The Balm in Gilead
He has far removed my hurt and healed all wounds.
He reached deep within me and from the sickness of sin He recovered me.
To full health He restored me. He has clothed me and given me a
righteous mind.

Dayspring from on High
Dawn of Salvation; by Him the light has sprung forth, the Sun has risen
in the hearts of men.
He has caused blinded eyes to see Truth, and the lost to find their way.
Light of Hope; by Him all confusion is overturned and peace ensues.
He reveals an expected finish, a certain victory.

The embodiment of God's agape' LOVE
He is the fullness of God's mercy and grace
Bringing reconciliation of God's people to Him.

Author and Finisher
Equal to God
The beginning and the end;
My destiny is secure in Him.

Master Teacher
He is the Master, teaching!
His knowledge is complete and entire.
His word is living authority.
His lectures are eternal.

The First and the Last
In the beginning was the Word.
That same Word will have the final say.

Aaron's Rod
Though cut off from His source, it was temporal.
He returned to life, rose to Heaven;
And there He stands
Chosen of God to make petitions for us
To secure the promise.

Royal Authority
Son of God
Heir to the Throne
Yet the epitome of humility and obedience

The Amen
The Faithful one
He finished what no man was qualified to do.

First Born of the Dead, He that Liveth and was Dead
Jesus died spiritually in our stead,
Conquered the darkness,
Returned to life with total power, glorified!
By it, we have been granted access to the same.

The Beginning of Creation
Restores man back to his place in God.

The Arm of the Lord
The authority of Almighty God
Made visible to the eyes of men.

The Sun of Righteousness
The illumination of God's glory to the hearts of men
He exposes that which is hidden;
Cancels darkness; and Lights the way.

My Kinsman Redeemer
My relations with the Father restored,
Mine was an insurmountable debt impossible to pay;
With riches untold, the lien on my life, He lifted;
He, for me, recovered all.

Bishop of My Soul
My supreme supervisor
Looks upon me with high regard,
My well-being to secure,

The Ultimate Sacrifice
As my Friend, He shed blood that will never lose its power
And He became my Savior.

The New Wine
Bringing divine healing and joy

Zion's Hill
In Him the children of my God dwell high
Above the reach of conflict and travail.
He is that gradient of grace
Out of whom our salvation comes.

The Sure Foundation
Fortified and not easy to be broken.
Upon which, a house built shall not fall.

Root out of the Stem of Jesse
To Him this branch is securely attached
He is my life source
In never-ending supply

Sweet Savor of Truth
The end of my captivity.
Thank you, Lord
By Him, I know that the devil is a liar, the perpetrator and author of
deceit.
Thank You
For Truth who stands a perfect opposite—beautiful, radiant Truth!

Faithful and True Witness
His witness was of Himself
He is The Way, the Truth and the Life.

The Chief Corner Stone
A stone, a tried stone;
The precious corner stone;
My anchor; my stronghold;
In Him I stand.

Sweet Manna from Heaven
He fills me up to satisfying.
Even from the deep reaches of my soul
He nourishes me.

My Peace Offering
By whom, Encouraged,
I come with confidence before the throne of my God.

The Stone of Ebenezer
He is my Ebenezer, God my help.
In the power of His name, the enemy is crushed.
He redeemed my failure, changed my destiny, and bought me the victory.

Frankincense
A priceless treasure of refreshing fragrance
Saturates my worship
Causing it to go before the Father
A satisfying sacrifice; a certifiable praise!

He that shutteth and *no man openeth*,
Conquered death, hell, and the grave.
He reigns victorious!

CHRIST CENTERED

Often, while driving an hour to work, I pray, mediate, and petition God. One particular morning, however, my spirit was fixed on nothing but praise. Each time I attempted to move to prayer, I found myself back to praise. It felt good! So, there I settled and was amazed at what the Holy Spirit, by this determined praise, poured out of me.

I began to tell Jesus all those things about Him that made Him the center and focus of my life. As the descriptives flowed, I felt compelled to pen them. Post my praise and for another three days, I continued my recording efforts before finally resting on the items that make up this praise.

Later, I attempted to stretch the Holy Spirit for more, but nothing came. "Okay, Lord. Let me count them and see if you are done with me." Forty, I counted and knew it was complete. Understand, forty is the age at which I declared to be exclusive with my Jesus, allowing Him to be the solitary source and center of me.

May you be recharged, refreshed, driven, and consumed to the point that nothing and no one can ever fill His space in you.

CHRIST CENTERED
(May 2013)

Source of my Adoration
Object of my Praise
Aim of my Worship
Provender of my Intake
Treasure of my Whispers
Thesis of my Lexis
Point of my Exclamations
Keystone of my Decrees
Cache of my Orations
Genius of my Excerpts
Core of my Edicts
Topic of my Expositions
Focus of my Emotions
Merit of my Citations
Center of my Exaltations
Heart of my Adulations
Objective of my Depositions
Pedestal of my High Regard
Crown of my Laughter
Axis of my Victory

Might of my Acclamations
Force of my Liberation
Celebrity of my Rapture
Priceless Fortune of my Explorations
Sound of my Shout
Theme of my Publications
Star Attraction of my Proclamations
Text/Intrigue of my Lectures
Substance of my Spoken Word
Worth of my Compilations
Headline of my Broadcasts
Philosophy of my Quotations
Frankincense of my Inhale
Emancipation of my Exhale
Subject of my Impenitent Bravado
Channel of my Communications
Dialogue of my Discourse
Tune of my Lyrical Exhortation
Imprint of my Expressions
Illumination of my Illustrations

HALLOWED BE THY NAME, JESUS!

During the 90's my quest for knowledge of and desire for intimacy with God's word became an interesting affair. The Word of God was so alluring that I found myself sitting in Sunday School, Bible Training Union, Mission, even Sunday Church service getting excited about some term or scripture that sparked my interest. In those moments, I knew that I had to dissect it more. The next couple of days would be spent generating detailed writings from material assembled using the Bible, Bible dictionary, concordance, standard dictionary as my research sources.

On one such occasion, the term hallowed became my intrigue. Untold recitation of "The Lord's Prayer" did not yield immediate understanding of the word 'hallowed' (Matthew 6:9). It dawned that common to me was a word expressed thousands of times across my life, yet its meaning I never considered.

A dictionary search of the word 'hallowed' evolved to this from God. From this time forth, when praying The Lord's Prayer, let your heart and mind return to its 'hallowed' meanings and all that it captures for you. **Let it bring excitement and joy**!!!

Hallowed Be Thy Name, Jesus!
(Matthew 6:9, October 1997 thru June 2011)

At the name of Jesus, Every knee shall bow, of things in heaven, in earth, and beneath the earth; and every tongue shall confess that He is Lord!

Owner and Author of my salvation,
Jesus secured from God a name above any other;
…The ram in the bush
…The Lamb
…The perfect, unblemished, faultless sacrifice

Unsurpassed in every way, shape, form or fashion
The incomparable name of Christ is:
…Sanctified
…Consecrated
…Holy

Supreme is His name— for He is indeed the reigning, conquering King!
Superlative is thy name.
…Untouchable
…Unreachable
…Undeniably awesome

Oh, how marvelous is thy name in all the earth;
Oh, how I love calling on that name, **Jesus!**
…Awesome
…Magnificent
…Amazing

Thy name is super beyond the natural.
To be exalted above all the earth;
…Glorious
…Peerless
…Praiseworthy

I hallow thy name, Jesus! **I make Thy name large!**

SWEET AND HOLY DOVE

At this point, well represented by the writings that I had accumulated over the years were the Father and the Son; not of the Holy Spirit, the one source of my ability to connect with them. He is the one who accompanies me on this earth while my Savior is away making preparations. He is with me, unconditionally 24-7, setting the temple of my God in order, preparing me for His return. Tirelessly, He puts up with my every flaw while lovingly perfecting me in my God's Truth—in Jesus.

I owe a great debt to my faithful companion. The following is a tribute to Him and all that He is to me; the least I can give in His honor.

By this, come what may, remember—in every failure and success—that you have a constant, unconditional support actively living and operating to perfect you; and on Him may you lean.

SWEET AND HOLY DOVE
(July 2011)

Father,
Thank You for Your Word;
Thank You for the Holy Spirit, the Light of Your Truth;
The Light that yields recognition, comprehension, and revelation of Truth.

The Light is…

The presence of God **indwelling** *me*	*In the deep reaches of my heart He takes residence. By Him, this tabernacle, my God occupies.*
The Son of God **embodying** *me*	*By Him, Jesus causes Himself to be in a multitude of nations at once, personally performing "greater works" through the flesh of inferior man.*
The power of God **endowing** *me*	*He issues out from the altar of the Master; the anointed presence and authority of Almighty God to put down all that oppose Him.*
The seal of God **preserving** *me*	*The divine policy holder, He provides paid-up, active, premium insurance and is guarantor of my redemption at the last day.*
The comfort of God **soothing** *me*	*He leads me to the Master's rest. Under the blanket of my God's peace, He covers me.*
The revelation of God **enlightening** *me*	*He exposes to me the righteousness of my God and reveals to my heart hidden things of the Kingdom…for members only.*

The anointing of God **overflowing** *me*	*Like a river, He floods my soul and releases a wave of God's provision. I'm healed by the Spirit of God's truth filling my heart.*
The staff of God **propping** *me*	*He is given to be a leaning post; enabling me to endure my cross.*
The oil of God **consecrating** *me*	*In the priesthood of Aaron I'm assigned to be. He prepares me in holiness and purity; separated unto God, His will in me to fulfill.*
The administrator of God **gifting** *me*	*In Kingdom-building, He assigns my purpose. By His unctioning, my desires are satisfied and the purpose of my God is made alive in me.*
The staff of God's Word **engrafting** *me*	*By promoting in me an abounding Gospel and blood-bought testimony, I triumph in excellence over the devices of the enemy.*
The waters of God **immersing** *me*	*By Him, the desert in me is made fertile; It is filled with the doctrine of God's Word bearing fruits of righteousness to build the Kingdom of God.*
The compass of God **guiding** *me*	*He directs me to things more excellent than this world. To Heaven's throne, He bids me see.*
The voice of God **moving** *me*	*A constant reminder of Truth, He leads me, without fail, to the Father's will. In the mind of God, He regulates my thoughts so that I walk in God.*
The breath of God **quickening** *me*	*By His transforming power, in new life, I've been raised. Through Him, a second birth attained; a new name to claim.*

The burning of God **pressing** me	Neither silent nor still can I be; for through me, the gospel story He reveals.
The perfection of God **maturing** me	He is the source of God's increase in me.
The warden of God **imprisoning** me	On lock-down, I humbly submit, in obedience, my steps ordered by God.
The school master of God **chastening** me	With the sweetness of the Savior's voice, He corrects me. A chastising made pure by His love that pierces my heart and leads me contrite before His throne.
Leader of the host of God **pursuing** me	As admiral in the siege; He causes my heart to surrender to God.
The sword of God **defending** me	Against the attacks of the enemy, He, my armor bearer; stands without fail as my cover and secures me.
The water of baptism **resurrecting** me	By Him, my old self has been buried and in Christ arisen anew.
My liberator **releasing** me	He leads me through victory's door where, in Truth, I find my refuge. Against sin, He is my conquistador.
The great deliberator **orating** me	He gives witness by my mouth to the awesomeness of Almighty God and the Truth of the Gospel of His Christ.
A member of the Elite **indoctrinating** me	He is my access to their table. All that I need to stand before my enemies, this table supplies.

The superior scholar **instructing** *me*	*He, of complete knowledge, makes plain Messiah's commands and equips me to walk in the plan. He is the only seal to authenticate my Master's decrees, for my God's Word, only He quickens alive in me.*
The faithful companion **accompanying** *me*	*Head-to-toe, above, below, round about me, inside and out, there is no hiding place. Everywhere I look causes my eyes to see Jesus. He is my constant help.*

A perfect and priceless treasure for my heart is that Sweet and Holy Dove.
He, the Jesus in me, the only good.

THE WATER IS TURNED TO WINE...

For prospective teachings at our church, the Pastor assigned me to do a biblical study of the Pharisee spirit. In preparation for the study, I pulled out my KJV bible CDs and listened while driving to and from work. Beginning with the Gospel of Matthew, of course, I quickly moved through successive CDs until John. This CD, from which I could not move, continued through John, chapter 9. Over and over, I played it and humbly listened expecting to receive a revelation of its relation to the Pharisee study. My thoughts as voiced were "Master, there has to be something in here that You want me to give particular attention to. What is it?"

After a few days of listening to the CD repetitively, there it was. It was one of those ah-ha moments; a moment such as when your mind's eye catches a sparkle and registers value in the seemingly insignificant, inherited bauble that you have worn off and on for years as costume jewelry. Your great grandmother's ring bears more than sentimental value. It is priceless. A little nugget revealed by the flicker of Holy Ghost light—John 2:7-10, specifically verse 10.

The next couple of days I meditated on that portion of scripture 'til the revelation hit. *** This is exactly what God did from the Original Covenant to the establishment of the New***. Hallelujah! The latter is indeed greater, as is going from water to wine!

THE WATER IS TURNED TO WINE...
(July 2013)

*Jesus saith unto them, Fill the waterpots with water. And they filled them up to the brim. And he saith unto them, Draw out now and bear unto the governor of the feast. And they bare it. When the ruler of the feast had tasted the water that was made wine, and knew not whence it was: (but the servants who drew the water knew) the governor of the feast called the bridegroom. And saith unto him, "**Every man at the beginning doth set forth good wine; and when men have well drunk, then that which is worse; but thou hast kept the good wine until now.**" John 2:7-1*

WATER	WINE
When the **Law** and his taskmaster	Give way to Love and His **Grace**
When the temporal—**Happiness**	Becomes the unconditional—**Joy**
When **Moses,** deliverer of the law written on tablets	Gives place to **Jesus,** deliverer of the law written in hearts
When the physical picture of the **Old** Testament	Becomes the spiritual reality of the **New** Testament
When baptism with **Water,** the symbol	Evolves to a baptism with **Fire,** the literal
When symbolic and external **Purification**	Becomes Holy Ghost driven **Sanctification**
When the **Physical** weakness of the flesh	Submits to the **Spiritual** power of the Word
The limited **Former Rain**	Is replaced by the abundant and all sufficient **Latter Rain**
When the **Former** perishable **House**	Is changed to the **Latter** indestructible **House**
When wayward **Flesh**	Gives in to obedient **Spirit**
When the anointing **Oil**	Releases the power of the **Holy Spirit**

When **Manna** that fell from the **skies**	Is made manifest as the **Bread of Life** sent down from **Heaven**
When **Corruption**	Has put on **Incorruption**
When the **Sickness and Disease** of **Sin**	Meets the **Healing** waters of **Salvation**
When the **Common**	Is now **Set Apart and Peculiar**
When **Condemnation** of the innocent	Brings **Justification** for the guilty
When by **Judgment** a **Sentence** is rendered	Yet by **Mercy** it's commuted to a **Release**
When the **"Guilty"** plea	Renders a **"Not Guilty"** verdict
When that which is **Spoken** by the Word	Is **Created** (brought into existence) by the Word
When the **Written and Spoken** Word	Stepped on the scene as the **Living, Walking, Breathing** Word

II

THE KNOWLEDGE OF YOUR TRUTH IS MY CONSUMPTION

In the meadow, in the splendor of Your
Word, is a never-ending spring

*Guide my intake, Dear Lord, and in Truth let me take
my fill 'til your likeness my life reveals.*

Imagine Isaiah's physical reaction to his vision of the Savior referenced in Isaiah 6:1-8. As Isaiah's jaw dropped, he was floored. The beauty and brilliance of Jesus was so perfectly pure that it exposed Isaiah's filthiness. This righteous, godly man was about his routine, living no doubt contentedly and self-satisfied as is the case with many of us, especially Christians. The cares of this world and physical life routinely distract us and often take our focus. Yet, the host of heaven continuously, without fail are focused on Him.

At a point, my routine of early morning meditations and studies got off track. This, I agonized over. I so desired to do better, but even in my thoughts and meditations my daily activities, struggles, and interfaces prevailed. Though I was ashamed for my neglect and sorrowful to God, still I failed.

In time, strength waned while struggles and failures that should never have been ensued. So amazing is the unfeigned love of the Master. As I sit typing and reflecting, in the spirit, I see Him smiling and stroking me in the midst of it all. My God has been longsuffering, kind, merciful, gracious even toward me. Love that is not bitter, puffed up, or shifting has been His stay. Just as He sent the seraphim with the live coal to purge and cleanse Isaiah, the coals are made ready to cleanse our iniquities. In the span of time, He exposes Himself to us in a new way drawing us back and bringing us again to His feet. There He can do what He desires most—spend time with us. Love was at hand as the struggles and tests that He allowed to come drew my focus back to Him, back consistently to my knees.

Our God never gives up on us. He is poised to take us back, to deliver us at our request. It is not for Him that He desires we remember Him. He stands solid; the majority and authority in all things. Rather, He knows that it is only in Him that you and I can stand. We are nothing without Him. Every day we wake; every night we lay; and every moment we have between, may we approach the cares of our lives with God on our minds unceasingly.

REMEMBER ME?
(December 2008)

In Your strength, we are lifted from our slumber.
You embrace us lovingly
Then, reach out and touch us with the dew upon our feet
Even when we fail to say "Good morning" to you.

In the flickering of the stars, you wink at us.
You wave sweetly through the gentle swaying of the trees
Then touch us gently with the cool breeze of the night
Even when we fail to bow and pray before slumbering.

In the failure to take time for you, our faces reveal the excess.
Still You smile upon us through the purity of the clouds and the shelter
of the heavens;
And warmly kiss our foreheads with the light of the sun
Though, we fail to take time for You amidst the activity of our day.

In each raindrop released, My God, You shower us with your love.
We become soaked in your mercy and your grace;
Though we are spoiled with luxuries of this world
And soiled with selfish acts of the flesh that put you on hold.

In the deep swaying calm of the ocean waves, you speak "Peace".
The rain ceases and the sun returns to kiss our foreheads.
To our hearts, you softly sing a new song as the birds whistle a tune.
Though, in spite of it all, we go on living like we do.

Then, within the span of time,
You lovingly braise us with the troubles of this world.
All the while, propping us up by the power of Your Word...lest we fall
Pressing us 'til we find that sweet release.

With it all, simply, you lovingly and gently ask,
"Remember Me?"
Thank You, Lord!
We shall **ever** remember Thee.

KINGDOM MINDED

A few years ago, while attending a funeral for a relative's husband, I reviewed the itinerary and unbeknownst to me my name was on it. With a short time to prepare, I asked God what He would have me say to His people so that we begin to look at ourselves through His eyes for a change as we journey through this life on our way home. He responded, "Tell them this." Paint a picture. "I'm looking down from my throne into a crowd of people and you are in the midst. How do I know that you belong to me?"

What does He find us doing? How does He find us acting? What does He hear us saying? Whatever or however, is it 'royal' or is it 'common'? That is the question. Christian believers need to understand that we are royalty even from the worldly operation of kingship and should stand out; never submitting to what is 'common'. Too many Christians, He said, operate compromised, carnal, in works alone, and in selfish ambitions of the flesh. We, in peace with the world, allow culturalism, elitism, even racism to be the rule. We must know that God, our Father the King, is grieved within us. Not that He loses anything by it; but that we miss out on a multitude of opportunity to change the world and to receive the blessings He so graciously desires to impart to us.

The end times are upon us. Now, more than ever, we must face our duty and walk in it. "Who do you represent?" When my children where at an early age, God laid this on my heart to ask whenever they get off track and those things not representative of the kingdom such as selfishness, discontentment, and yelling rise up in them. My sincere belief is that God wants us to draw on this question and to search our heart regarding every action, conversation, and thought.

Ever considered how awesome it is to be saved? Adopted into the family of Abraham out of which came great kings? We are now royal, of noble blood, the blood of Jesus; and heirs, joint heirs with Christ.

Our Father is King. As princes [and princesses], we are charged to build, establish, advocate/promote His kingdom.

On this earth, reigning kingdoms are set apart. The attire stands out; it is respectful, modest, of the finest quality. Verbal communication is intelligent, full of humility, carefully censored. Posture is erect, assured, and confident. Their temperament is authoritative, controlled, and mellow. Though association is guarded, select, and limited, they influence a multitude. They set the standard—a peculiar people, separated and set apart from the world; not conformed to it, but purposed to conform it to the kingdom. They had the authority to execute, to direct, and to command alignment with the king's decrees. They had access to the king's signet [in our Father's Kingdom it is the name of Jesus] which authorized them to make their declarations sure; to the subjection of the citizens of the kingdom and the conquered.

In the years since this perspective of royalty and what it should mean to us to be children of the King, God has given much more. Many pages I have written covering this subject. Recently, I asked God for a poem to provide a simple, quick synopsis of it. Otherwise, it would amount to an excess, a book of rhetoric. The result follows.

KINGDOM MINDED
(May 2011)
Sons of God, Sons of the King:

Know not that you are royalty?
How can this be?
With Your Father's enemies, you've made friends.
In their filth and rags, you've invited them in.
You've even traded your royal robe for their attire.
And by it, you've made my God a liar.

Know not that you are royalty?
No compromise can there be.
Now set your sights as the wise;
And in Him rise,
Peculiar, separated, set apart,
To draw them to His heart.

Know not that your Father is King?
To Him only your sacrifices bring.
All of you,
Nothing less will do.
Only in His purity,
Can any success be?

Know not that your Father is King?
His kingdom you must get building.
Boldly walk in the authority;
For with Him, you are the majority.
Make His enemies your footstool,
By His prevailing rule.

You are Royalty, indeed;
For, "yes", Your Father is King!
It is your destiny; your responsibility;
And it is your legacy,
To "live" the gospel story,
That He may bring many sons to Glory.

My prayer is this:

Let your kingdom building begin in me, Lord God.

Thy kingdom come to my heart, Jesus.
Rest, rule, and abide there; and lord over me.

Search me and know me, O' Lord; and
renew your righteous Spirit in me.

Strengthen me where I'm weak.
Build me up and fortify me where I am torn down.
Cleanse every stubborn stain and
Straighten every crooked way that remains in me.
Chisel out the rough places and make them smooth.
Mold me.
Shape me.
Make me fit for your use.

So, that I not attach myself to anything that is not attached to you, God,

Build your kingdom in me;
First, in me…

MOST GRATEFUL

When pondering my life and the heart that I have acquired for Jesus, everything I consider, everything I see, everything that is good, comes back to Jesus. Everything that is in me, every desire that I have for Him is given, imparted to me by Him.

I am so grateful and so humbled that He designed me and put inside me an affinity for Him. Most grateful that he reached way down into the muck and the mire, retrieved it, and pulled it out of me to make my life useful to Him.

This is not of me. It is of the grace and predestination of Almighty God that I am in this place. I would but that I not fail Him. By His gracious provision, I know with a resounding truth that:

I am a wretch, indeed, without Him. There is no good thing going on in this flesh BUT GOD!

MOST GRATEFUL
I am so grateful.

You saw fit to shine Your Light in my direction, and thankfully you did not stop there.
Still you opened my eyes and
Allowed me to look upon it
Caused me to see it
Conditioned my mind to comprehend it
In prelude to it all, you tenderly prepared my heart to receive the Light of Your Truth and at my asking, you readily filled me with it.

In me, the Light has become the burning that purges and constantly purifies me.
It pierces forth out of me
To invite your presence in Worship
To exclaim your praises in Song
To witness your Truth in Testimony
Jesus, on the inside in a multitude of places at once, performs the "greater works" through the flesh of inferior man.

I am grateful, most grateful!

LORD, GOD
Your Word is…

During college, God harnessed my thirst for Him and His Truth by putting fellow and devout Christian schoolmates in my path. My level of faith, knowledge, and spiritual awareness grew tremendously from participation in many Bible study groups and attendance at varied churches— Baptist, Church of God in Christ, Non-denominational, white pastors, black pastors, television evangelists.

In the late 90's, God took me through another process of educating me in His Word. For a period of time, He would wake me daily between 2:30 to 4:30 a.m. Burning in me was a thirst and hunger for Him and His truths that I had not experienced since college. This writing evolved out of that period.

God excited my quest for knowledge through varied arenas—television, evangelism, public speakers, conferences, standard church services, songs. Name it. God would stir me in some way by anything that had something to do with Him. My writings were born out of everything from simple dictionary word searches to inspirational readings to short documents of revelation to detailed research papers.

Then, God poured His Truths into me as I had never known before. He gave me revelations that manifested in my heart long before I read them in the scriptures. These days, I hear the voice of my God when I'm immersed in reading His Word almost exclusively. So, when I ask for answers, agonize, sweat, even pout, I seldom hear His voice except through the scriptures. When I open up the Bible, at the instant I begin to read, I hear clearly as He begins to speak and our conversation begins to unfold. Through the pages of His Word, He stimulates me; He stirs me; He reveals Himself to me.

In one phase of my quest for knowledge, God spoke these exact words to me "Take my yoke upon you". Matter of course, I looked up the scripture source and read the entire periscope. Pondering "…and learn of me" particularly, I concluded that it meant I needed to read through the four gospels and through them walk out the life of Jesus on earth. For some reason which I could not make sense of at the time, I kept drifting away from those New Testament books and was drawn strongly by the things written in the Old Testament. Beginning at Genesis, I read through to the Kings and some of both Isaiah and Ezekiel. I could not rationalize nor relinquish the unexplainable magnetic pull of these writings. Though out of it came much revelation from God, I felt guilty for going off-track of what I believed to be His direction when He commanded, "Take my yoke upon you."

Then one day, while apologizing to God, I realized that He had drawn me to the Old Testament. That, indeed, I was where I was supposed to be and learning of my Savior as directed. All became clear and my peace returned as Jesus spoke, "This is my yoke. All scripture point to me."

Thinking one day on these great opportunities at knowledge and the great provisions God made for me through His Word, I jotted some down.

God gave me His Word; and by it, He gave me Jesus.

LORD, GOD
Your Word is...

Powerful	Matthew 17:20	It moves mountains.
Invincible	Matthew 24:35	It stands sure.
Radiant	I John 1:5	Darkness cannot dwell in its midst.
Penetrating	Hebrew 4:12	It settles in the deep reaches of my being.
True	John 8:32	It sets hearts and minds free
Sufficient	Matthew 4:4	Bread of Heaven; It feeds me until I am full.
Fulfillment	Psalm 107:9; Matthew 5:6	It dwells within us.
Comforting	John 14:7	It speaks 'peace' to me.
Charity	I Corinthians 13:4-8a	It abounds in Love.
Liberating	Psalm 23:5b	It fills my cup to overflowing.
Timeless	Galatians 5:14	It is the fulfillment of the Old in the New.
Compassionate	Lamentations 3:22; Psalm 51:1	It sheds the tenderest mercies.
Alive	John 1:1-4	It became flesh and dwelt among us.
Life	Proverb 4:20-22	It issues forth through the spiritual Realm to release physical life, health, and longevity.
Provision	I Timothy 5:17	It is my trainer and the source of my supply.
Quickening	Psalm 119:50; 1Peter 3:18	It, put to death by my sins, rose again in me; and caused me to live in Jesus, Free.
Eternal	John 3:16; John 17:2-3	It influences me in the Truth that I may lay hold on everlasting life

AVAILABLE

"Prayer changes things."
"Little prayer, little power;"
"Much prayer, much power."

The above quotes I have heard numerous times. The purpose and design is to promote prayer, a critical element of Christianity. In our walk and relationship with God, prayer is one area where many of us find ourselves most fallible and slothful. Knowing that it is necessary to our spiritual strength, we, frustratingly, seem to have a difficult time with this. We are guilty of falling asleep on God; the bed is so enticing that we can't leave it to get on our knees. Perhaps feeling unworthy due to recent failures, allowing cares of the world and activities of our lives to interrupt, whichever, whatever, our infidelities in this arena of our walk with God are many.

Getting to a place of consistency and faithfulness in prayer is a wrestling match against principalities set up by the enemy. Set up to drive us away from this significant source of strength. You see, Satan knows that he can't have us. The moment that you and I accepted Jesus Christ as our Lord and Savior our liberty was established securely—settled in Heaven forever. From the damnation of sin, we were released. Heaven became our home and we were sealed forever by the Holy Spirit. Furthermore, the Master makes it clear that none can pluck us from His Hand.

Denied control of (no longer controlling) our physical and spiritual being, all the enemy can attempt to devour, rob, kill and destroy is our witnes0000s and effectiveness for the Kingdom. By keeping us from praying, the enemy effectively keeps us from tuning in to God's voice, hearing Him more clearly, increasing our knowledge of His will, gaining strength, and securing balance, solace and rest. During a period of unemployment; I found myself in this struggle, again.

Needing desperately to focus, embrace this opportunity, and seek from God direction and strength, I wrote "Available" which follows.

It is a personal reflection of a grave need for prayer, cultivation of my relationship with the Master, and navigation through the current muck and mire to God's purpose on the other side of my storm.

Be inspired to push against the principalities of the enemy that are designed to keep us from the lover of our souls and cause us to miss the pleasures and empowerment of relationship with Him.

AVAILABLE
(August 2010)

My availability to You…
Affirms my existence; I am nothing without You.
Breathes new life; I am dead without You.
Causes truth to rest on me; I will believe a lie without You.
Dispenses Your grace through me; I would know no mercy without You.
Engrafts Your Word in me; my speech is vain without You
Fortifies me with power; I have no might without You.
Guarantees my help; I am overwhelmed without You

Hallows Your sovereignty God; I would serve idols without You.
Imparts worth; I am a wretch without You.
Justifies my value; I am worthless without You.

Kindles Your perfect strength; I am weak without You
Lights my path; I am in darkness without You.
Maps my way; I am lost without You.
Nets favor; in my praise is Your habitation.
Offers a lamp unto my feet; I am confused and have no direction without You.
Provides for my escape; I would succumb to temptation without You.

Qualifies my hold on eternal life; I have no faith without You.
Reveals a clear path; I will stumble without You.
Sets me apart; I am common without You.

Tenders my security; by Your Holy Spirit, I am sealed in You.
Unifies the three parts of me, I am out of order without You.
Validates my completeness; I am void without You.
Witnesses Your Truth; I would be in bondage without You.
X-tinguishes all traces of sin in me, I would be condemned without You…
Yields fruit; I am useless without You.
Zips my victory, BECAUSE YOU WERE FIRST AVAILABLE TO ME!

I am available to You.
You and me, Jesus; for I am not whole without You.

WITNESS

I am at a place in my life where I just want to experience GOD. Focused, I deliberately seek Him especially in those things that are quickly taken for granted or often simply overlooked.

One day and for a period of time thereafter, I found myself pondering, "How to deal with people who refuse to accept that God exists because they are engulfed by the evolution theory and/or entrenched in an environment of the opposite influence such as atheism; horrible experiences from childhood, etc.?" I was deeply concerned that some people possibly may never chance hearing the gospel because the odds are stacked against them.

Of course, the need for a 'physical, human' witness was where my thoughts centered. Understand that my heart had already connected to the fact that God is 'everything'. To this truth, the Holy Spirit ministered, "They do have a witness. I have placed a witness of myself in everything that I created." Literally, I began to look for God's witness of Himself in all His creation. On the long drive to work, I simply looked and thought on the things of nature while listening for the Spirit to remind me of scripture or reveal something new about the things I noticed day to day. To you, I boast in God that the scriptural revelations about the things of nature that you are about to read were more than ¾ unfamiliar to me in the light which God's Spirit gave during this period of my meditations.

Still concerned after weeks of pondering and the Spirit's revelations complete, I appealed, "Lord, what if I am off on some of the things I have written? I didn't hear you right? I was thinking out of my flesh?" I could feel the Spirit smirking with confidence within me as He expressed, "Search the scriptures." Needless to say, the Word witnessed in written form what God had revealed to my heart; over 80% of it was found to be backed by scripture. Certainly, it's just a matter of time before the others reveal themselves as well. Until then, I bid, "Let the Spirit be your witness to their truth."

Of these WITNESSES, the Holy Word of God puts it this way:

For the invisible things of him from the creation of the world are clearly seen, being understood by the things that are made, even his eternal power and Godhead; so that they are without excuse.

Romans 1:20

Can I get a witness?
Who will stand and testify?

WITNESS
Even the elements witness the existence of Almighty God.
(October 2010)

For by him were all things created, that are in heaven, and that are in earth, visible and invisible, whether they be thrones, or dominions, or principalities, or powers: all things were created by him, and for him: Colossians 1:16

"All of God's creation function to witness the abiding presence of Almighty God".

The sun illuminates the Glory of God and the Righteousness of Jesus.	John 5:35; Revelation 18:1; Malachi 4:2
The light of the sun expresses His Truth.	John 3:19; I Timothy 6:16
The darkness of the night reminds us that our lives will expire someday.	John 9:4
The rising of the sun reflects the transition from sin to salvation, from death to life.	1 Peter 2:9
The moon lights up the sky to remind us that Jesus is that light in the midst of darkness.	2 Corinthians 4:6; Isaiah 9:2; Psalm 18:28
The stars represent the multitude of saints on this earth and who shall be around the throne praising God.	Deuteronomy 10:22; Psalm 148:3; Revelation 1:20
The sky never ends. It is above us wherever we go. This is the omnipresence of Almighty God. The universe displays the awesomeness and vastness of the mind and wisdom of God.	Psalm 139:8

The vastness and expansion of the galaxies attest to the far-reaching power of Almighty God and stand as a testament of His boundless grace and endless mercies.

The wind expresses the force of God's all-might which was used to push back and part the red sea.	Acts 2:2; Isaiah 11:15b; Exodus 10:13 & 14:21; Psalm 78:26 & 48:7
The clouds show forth God as our covering, our strength, and our protection.	Exodus 14:20; 24, 25
Dew affirms the favor of the Lord and that there is a fresh supply of His tender mercies every day.	Psalm 19:12 & 133:3
The grass reminds us of the shortness of this life. It flourishes; yet expires quickly.	Psalm 72:16 & 103:15; Isaiah 40:6-8 & 51:12; Job 10:20 & 14:1
Mature trees exemplify lives anchored and rooted in God, producing fruits of righteousness	Psalm 1

"Words cannot sufficiently express the magnitude of God's excellence. Yet, He has fashioned the ever-present elements to express His Glory where we cannot."

Regarding the all-powerful, unattainable, awestruck wonders of our God, I'm reminded of recent natural disasters and how they have impacted the entire world. God says: "My Glory is in that too."

The rain reveals the outpouring of His Word and saturation <u>in</u> His Word to fill and satisfy our hearts after His good pleasure. It reminds us of Jesus, the "Bread of Heaven" who feeds, nourishes, and strengthens our spirit man. — Exodus 16:4

The lightening is demonstrative of the far reaching power of All-mighty God and flashes to reveal the swift two-edge sharpness of the Word of God. — Job 37:3; Zechariah 9:14

Thunder serves to remind us the end is imminent, at which time the trumpet will sound and all will hear. — Job 37:4, 5

The disturbances in the atmosphere—such as thunderstorms, tornadoes, floods, hurricanes, typhoons, volcanic eruptions, forest fires, monsoons, earthquakes, tsunamis, and the like—all serve to remind us that the wrath and judgment of God is certain. — Isaiah 29:6 & 30:30; Psalm 11:6 & 83:15; 2 Peter 2:17

The seasons and change of seasons are there to remind us not to become complacent and content with this earth; not to attach ourselves to it; that this life is not meant to last forever; we are sojourners designed strictly for the Master's purpose and His Glory. — 1Chronicles 29:15; Ecclesiastes 3:1

All God's creation exclaiming: "The Kingdom of Heaven is at hand! Prepare ye the way of the Lord!"

The seas (many waters) are witness of the fullness, quickening, and filling of the Holy Spirit, God's never-ending supply. It satisfies.

Proverbs 25:25; John 7:38; Song of Solomon 4:15;

The mountains extenuate the abiding presence, the holiness, and the unquenchable joy of our God.

Psalm 125:1,2 & 148:1

The vast and awe-inspiring landscapes of this earth reveal God, the Master Artist.

The roundness of the earth witnesses God's infinity; There is no place of its beginning or its end; It reminds us of a God who is the beginning and the end, the ancient of days.

The division of the earth in two hemispheres such that one is experiencing day, while the other experiences night reveals the separation of light from darkness, the wheat from the tares. This shall be the condition of the earth at judgment, separation of the sinners from the righteous.

Jewels, precious stones, and the rarest of treasures enlighten. They serve to remind us of the precious gifts of God-His coming kingdom [the New Jerusalem] laden with priceless elements and the greatest treasure of all, salvation. Jesus is our salvation. He gives beauty for ashes and the oil of joy for mourning.

1 Corinthians 3:11; Matthew 13:14; Revelation 21:19

"Let us give Him a perfect praise; who has made us to be a voice of praise to Him in the earth."

The sheep is an impressively submissive animal, yet easily confused and lost without the constant watchful eye and guidance of a shepherd. It serves to remind us of our frailty and inadequacy without Jesus, the good shepherd.

Isaiah 53:6; John 10:11, 14

The strength of an eagle enables it to travel from one end of the earth to the other. It is able to see at magnitudes unsurpassed by other living creatures. All-seeing is our God. There is nothing hidden from Him. His eyes go to and fro the earth trying the hearts of men and showing Himself strong to the heart that is perfect toward Him.

2 Chronicles 16:9

The lamb is a meek and humble animal to remind us of Jesus who was the express representation of God's love manifest in the flesh and who without complaint laid down his life to damnation in our stead that we might be delivered from the eternal judgment. He became our Savior.

Isaiah 53:7; Revelation 5:6 & 14:1; I John 4:10; I Peter 1:18,19

The Lion is powerful. Considered the most dominant of animals, it is exclaimed 'king of the jungle' to remind us of a Savior who is: King of kings, Lord of lords, Wonderful, Counselor, Prince of Peace, Everlasting Father, The Mighty God—Lion of the Tribe of Judah!

Revelation 5:4,5; Isaiah 31:4 & 9:6, 7; I Timothy 6:15

Reflecting on all God's creation, I remember in the book of Genesis that later on the 6th day, God personally and meticulously crafted and breathed life into His final creation. You see, the makeup of man is the likeness of God on the earth—a trinity, 3-in-1—mind, body, soul. (little gods)

Genesis 1:26, 27; 5:1

What's more, the makeup of the human body reveals God, the Master engineer.

Psalm 139:13-16;
Genesis 1:27; 2:7

Further, I am reminded that at the end of each of the first 5 days of creation, God looked back on all that He had made and, Genesis says, He saw that it was "good". At the end of the sixth day, God looked backed on all that He had created, which now included man and, Genesis concludes, He upgraded what saw to a status of "very good".

As God's greatest and most proud creation, I refuse to let the birds so sweetly whistle a tune and fail to sing my God's praises. Unto his praise, neither will valleys bow nor will mountains extend without me. So, I commit. As the powerful songstress, CeCe Winans put it, "I join with all nature in manifold witness." For great is my God's faithfulness toward me!

Alone He is God! And Alone He is Worthy!

WANTED

It was early 2011. Prior, in October 2010, a fellow church member and I volunteered to serve as table hosts for Broadmoor Baptist Church's upcoming 'Women's Night Out' event assigned the theme 'Lasso Your Legacy'. As hosts, our responsibilities were to decorate an assigned table with personal items reflecting the theme and to host the ladies who would eat at that table. We brainstormed decorations, discussing and planning everything from bandanas to lanterns to cowboy hats, to even the mints for the bandana styled gift bags. That part was easy. The tough part came with our desire to present and impress 'Jesus' while keeping with the theme. How would we accomplish it?

I tell you, through the Holy Spirit for which I am so grateful. Through Him, I can ask God for help on anything especially that which is after His heart and I will get an answer. The answer came as an idea to do something analogous to 'wanted' posters depicting the thing wanted as some virtue of a woman in the Bible. In my mind, I began to walk through the Bible. From Genesis through the New Testament, I availed God to testify on behalf of the virtues He wanted depicted.

As well, we sought an overall scripture to sum the total of God's heart regarding the legacy He has determined for His children. The themed scripture became Psalm 16:5-6.

The Lord is the portion of mine inheritance and of my cup: thou maintainest my lot. The lines are fallen unto me in pleasant places; yea, I have a goodly heritage.

Listed are the virtues that evolved at the direction of the Holy Spirit.

WANTED

The Fruitfulness of Eve	Gen 3:20	And Adam called his wife's name Eve; because she was the mother of all living.
The Tenacity of Shiphrah and Puah	Ex 1:15, 17	And the king of Egypt spake to the Hebrew midwives, of which the name of the one was Shiphrah, and the name of the other Puah: But the midwives feared God, and did not as the king of Egypt commanded them, but saved the men children alive.
The Optimism of Moses' Mother	Ex 2:3	And when she could no longer hide him, she took for him an ark of bulrushes, and daubed it with slime and with pitch, and put the child therein; and she laid it in the flags by the river's brink.
The True Worship of Miriam	Ex 15:20	And Miriam the prophetess, the sister of Aaron, took a timbrel in her hand; and all the women went out after her with timbrels and with dances.
The Repentive Heart of Rahab	Josh 2:11	And as soon as we had heard these things, our hearts did melt, neither did there remain any more courage in any man, because of you: for the LORD your God, he is God in heaven above, and in earth beneath.
The Empowerment of Deborah	Judg 4:4	And Deborah, a prophetess, the wife of Lapidoth, she judged Israel at that time.

The Alliance of Jael	Judg 5:24, 26	Blessed above women shall Jael the wife of Heber the Kenite be, blessed shall she be above women in the tent. *She put her hand to the nail, and her right hand to the workmen's hammer; and with the hammer she smote Sisera, she smote off his head, when she had pierced and stricken through his temples.
The Adoption of Ruth	Ruth 1:16	And Ruth said, Entreat me not to leave thee, or to return from following after thee: for whither thou goest, I will go; and where thou lodgest, I will lodge: thy people shall be my people, and thy God my God:
The Restoration of Naomi	Ruth 1:42; 4:14,15	So Naomi returned, and Ruth the Moabitess, her daughter inlaw, with her, which returned out of the country of Moab: and they came to Bethlehem in the of barley harvest. * And the women said unto Naomi, Blessed be the LORD, which hath not left thee this day without a kinsman, that his name may be famous in Israel. *And he shall be unto thee a restorer of thy life, and a nourisher of thine old age: for thy daughter in law, which loveth thee, which is better to thee than seven sons, hath born him.
The Determination of Tamar	Ruth 4:12a [ref. Gen 8]	And let thy house be like the house of Pharez, whom Tamar bare unto Judah, of the seed which the LORD shall give thee

The Sacrifice of Hannah	1 Sam 1:28	Therefore also I have lent him to the LORD; as long as he liveth he shall lent to the LORD. And he worshipped the LORD there.
The Understanding of Abigail	1Sam 25:3a	Now the name of the man was Nabal; and the name of his wife Abigail: and she was a woman of good understanding, and of a beautiful countenance:
The Obedience of the Widow of Zarephath	1Kings 17:15	And she went and did according to the saying of Elijah: and she, and he, and her house, did eat many days.
The Compassion of the Little Maiden	2Kings 5:3	And she said unto her mistress, Would God my lord were with the prophet that is in Samaria! For he would recover him of his leprosy.
The Resolve of Esther	Esth 4:16	Go, gather together all the Jews that are present in Shushan, and fast ye for me, and neither eat nor drink three days, night or day: I also and my maidens will fast likewise; and so will I go in unto the king, which is not according to the law: and if I perish, I perish.
The Wisdom of King Lemuel's mother	Prov 31:1	The words of king Lemuel, the prophecy that his mother taught him.
The Virtue of "a woman who fears God"	Prov 31:31...	one who fears the Lord and departs from evil; who detaches herself from all things unlike God
The Ministry of Peter's Mother-n-Law	Matt 8:15	And he touched her hand, and the fever left her: and she arose, and ministered unto them.

The Confidence of the Woman with the issue of blood	Matt 9:21	For she said within herself, If I may but touch his garment, I shall be whole.
The Determination of the Canaanite woman	Matt 15:26-28	But he answered and said, It is not meet to take the children's bread, and to cast it to dogs. * And she said, Truth, Lord: yet the dogs eat of the crumbs which fall from their masters' table. * Then Jesus answered and said unto her, O woman, great is thy faith: be it unto thee even as thou wilt. And her daughter was made whole from that very hour
The Watchful Eye [or Readiness] of the 5 Wise Virgins	Matt 25:4, 10	But the wise took oil in their vessels with their lamps. *And while they went to buy, the bridegroom came; and they that were ready went in with him to the marriage: and the door was shut
The Selflessness of the Widow with the 2 mites	Mark 12:44	For all they did cast in of their abundance; but she of her want did cast in all that she had, even all her living.
The Favor of Mary, Mother of Jesus	Luke 1:28	And the angel came in unto her, and said, Hail, thou that art highly favored, the Lord is with thee: blessed art thou among women.
The Infilling of Elisabeth	Luke 1:41	And it came to pass, that, when Elisabeth heard the salutation of Mary, the babe leaped in her womb; and Elisabeth was filled with the Holy Ghost:

The Scholarship & Education of Mary, Sister of Martha	Luke 10:39,42	And she had a sister called Mary, which also sat at Jesus' feet, and heard his word. *But one thing is needful: and Mary hath chosen that good part, which shall not be taken away from her.
The Hospitality of Martha	Luke 10:40a	But Martha was cumbered about much serving
This Persistence of the Widow before the unjust judge	Luke 18:5-7	Yet because this widow troubleth me, I will avenge her, lest by her continual coming she weary me. *And the Lord said, Hear what the unjust judge saith. *And shall not God avenge his own elect, which cry day and night unto Him, though He bear long with them
The Discipleship of the Woman of Samaria	John 4:29	Come, see a man, which told me all things that ever I did: is not this the Christ?
The Liberty of Mary Magdalene	John 8:10, 11	When Jesus had lifted up himself, and saw none but the woman, he said unto her, Woman, where are those thine accusers? Hath no man condemned thee? * She said, No man, Lord. And Jesus said unto her, Neither do I condemn thee: go, and sin no more.
The Humility of Mary	John 12:3a	Then took Mary a pound of ointment of spikenard, very costly, and anointed the feet of Jesus, and wiped his feet with her hair:

The Servitude of Phebe	Rom 16:1, 2	I commend unto you Phebe our sister, which is a servant of the church which is at Cenchrea: *That ye receive her in the Lord, as becometh saints, and that ye assist her in whatsoever business she hath need of you: for she hath been a succourer of many, and of myself also.
The Listening Ear of Lydia	Acts 16:14	And a certain woman named Lydia, a seller of purple, of the city of Thyatira, which worshipped God, heard us: whose heart the Lord opened, that she attended unto the things which were spoken of Paul.
The Credentials of Priscilla	Acts 18:26...	And he began to speak boldly in the synagogue: whom when Aquila and Priscilla had heard, they took him unto them, and expounded unto him the way of God more perfectly.
The Prophecy of the Virgin Daughters	Acts 21:8b, 9	Philip the evangelist, which was one of the seven; and abode with him. *And the same man had four daughters, virgins, which did prophesy.
The Legacy of Lois and Eunice	II Timothy 1:5	When I call to remembrance the unfeigned faith that is in in thee, which dwelt first in thy grandmother Lois, and thy mother Eunice; and I am persuaded that in thee also.
The Faith of Sarah	Heb 11:11	Through faith also Sara herself received strength to conceive seed, and was delivered of a child when she was past age, because she judged him faithful who had promised.

The Preparation of the Bride of Jesus   Rev 19:7-9a   Let us be glad and rejoice, and give honor to him: for the marriage of the Lamb is come, and his wife hath made herself ready. * And to her was granted that she should be arrayed in fine linen, clean and white: for the fine linen is the righteousness of saints. * And he saith unto me, Write, Blessed are they which are called unto the marriage supper of the Lamb.

WANTED TOO
(September, 2013)

Really, the evolution of this one was uneventful. Inclusion of the men did not register on my radar screen until well after completing 'Wanted' and adding it to the initial draft of this book.

Following months of resisting the pressing of God to neutralize the imbalance, a compilation of biblical men evolved for intake/consumption. After all, God made man in His own image. Their spiritual make-up reveals God's face.

That's it. No sparks. No flames...

WANTED TOO

The Stewardship of Adam	Gen 2:15	And the LORD God took the man, and put him into the garden of Eden to dress it and to keep it.
The Excellency of Abel	Gen 4:4 Heb 11:4	And Abel, he also brought of the firstlings of his flock and of the fat thereof. And the LORD had respect unto Abel and to his offering: ; By faith Abel offered unto God a more excellent sacrifice than Cain, by which he obtained witness that he was righteous, God testifying of his gifts: and by it he being dead yet speaketh.
The Fruitfulness of Abraham	Gen 12:2	And I will make of thee a great nation, and I will bless thee, and make thy name great; and thou shalt be a blessing:
The Intimacy of Enoch	Gen 5:24	And Enoch walked with God: and he was not; for God took him.
The Longevity of Methuselah	Gen 5:27	And all the days of Methuselah were nine hundred sixty and nine years: and he died.
The Obedience of Noah	Gen 7:5	And Noah did according unto all that the LORD commanded him.
The Inheritance of Isaac	Gen 17:21	But my covenant will I establish with Isaac, which Sarah shall bear unto thee at this set time in the next year.
The New Name of Jacob	Gen 32:28	And he said, Thy name shall be called no more Jacob, but Israel: for as a prince hast thou power with God and with men, and hast prevailed.
The Prosperity of Joseph	Gen 39:3	And his master saw that the Lord was with him, and that the Lord made all that he did to prosper in his hand.

The Heritage of Judah	Gen 49:8-10	Judah, thou art he whom thy brethren shall praise: thy hand shall be in the neck of thine enemies; thy father's children shall bow down before thee. Judah is a lion's whelp: from the prey, my son, thou art gone up: he stooped down, he couched as a lion, and as an old lion; who shall rouse him up? The sceptre shall not depart from Judah, nor a lawgiver from between his feet, until Shiloh come; and unto him shall the gathering of the people be.
The Wisdom of Jethro	Exodus 18:14, 19-23	And when Moses' father in law saw all that he did to the people, he said, ... Why sittest thou thyself alone, and all the people stand by thee from morning unto even? ...Hearken now unto my voice I will give thee counsel, and God shall be with thee: Be thou for the people to God-ward, that thou mayest bring the causes unto God: ... Moreover, thou shall provide out of all the people, able men, such as fear the God, ...And let them judge the people at all seasons ... If thou shalt do this thing, and God command thee so, then thou shalt be able to endure, ... and they shall bear the burden with thee.

The Blessing of Aaron	Num 6:23-27	Speak unto Aaron and unto his sons, saying, On this wise ye shall bless the children of Israel, saying unto them, The LORD bless thee, and keep thee: The LORD make his face shine upon thee, and be gracious unto thee: The LORD lift up his countenance upon thee, and give thee peace. And they shall put my name upon the children of Israel; and I will bless them.
The Leadership of Moses	Num 12:7-8a	My servant Moses is not so, who is faithful in all mine house. With him will I speak mouth to mouth, even apparently, and not in dark speeches; and the similitude of the LORD shall he behold
The Confidence of Caleb	Num 14:38	But Joshua the son of Nun, and Caleb the son of Jephunneh, which were of the men that went to search the land, lived still.
The Conquering Might of Joshua	Josh 1:5	There shall not any man be able to stand before thee all the days of thy life: as I was with Moses, so I will be with thee: I will not fail thee, nor forsake thee.
The Valor of Gideon	Judg 6:12	And the angel of the LORD appeared unto him, and said unto him, The LORD is with thee, thou mighty man of valor.
The Resolve of Samson	Judg 16:30	And Samson said, Let me die with the Philistines. And he bowed himself with all his might; and the house fell upon the lords, and upon all the people that were therein. So the dead which he slew at his death were more than they which he slew in his life.

The Kinship of Boaz	Ruth 4:13,14	So Boaz took Ruth, and she was his wife: and when he went in unto her, the LORD gave her conception, and she bare a son. And the women said unto Naomi, Blessed be the LORD, which hath not left thee this day without a kinsman, that his name may be famous in Israel.
The Spiritual Ear of Samuel	II Sam 3:1,10	And the child Samuel ministered unto the LORD before Eli. And the word of the LORD was precious in those days; there was no open vision. And the LORD came, and stood, and called as at other times, Samuel, Samuel. Then Samuel answered, Speak; for thy servant heareth.
The Confidence of David	I Sam 17:45-47	Then said David to the Philistine, Thou comest to me with a sword, and with a spear, and with a shield: but I come to thee in the name of the Lord of hosts, the God of the armies of Israel, whom thou hast defied. This day will the Lord deliver thee into my hand; and I will smite thee, and take thine head from thee; and I will give the carcasses of the host of the Philistines this day unto the fouls of the air, and to the wild beasts of the earth; that all the earth may know that there is a God in Israel. And all will know that the Lord saveth not with sword and spear: for the battle is the Lord's, and He will give you into our hands.
The Brotherhood of Jonathan	I Sam 18:1	And it came to pass, when he had made an end of speaking unto Saul, that the soul of Jonathan was knit with the soul of David, and Jonathan loved him as his own soul.

The Rest of Solomon	I Kings 5:4	But now the Lord my God hath given me rest on every side, so that there is neither adversary nor evil occurrent
The Power of the Prayer of Solomon	I Kings 9:3	And the LORD said unto him, I have heard thy prayer and thy supplication, that thou hast made before me: I have hallowed this house, which thou hast built, to put my name there for ever; and mine eyes and mine heart shall be there perpetually.
The Unction of Jonathan	I Kings 14:6-8	And Jonathan said to the young man that bare his armour, Come, and let us go over unto the garrison of these uncircumcised: it may be that the LORD will work for us: for there is no restraint to the LORD to save by many or by few. And his armourbearer said unto him, Do all that is in thine heart: turn thee; behold, I am with thee according to thy heart. Then said Jonathan, Behold, we will pass over unto these men, and we will discover ourselves unto them.
The Faith of Elijah	I Kings 18:35, 38	And the water ran round about the altar; and he filled the trench also with water. Then the fire of the Lord fell, and consumed the burnt sacrifice, and the wood, and the stones, and the dust, and licked up the water that was in the trench.
The Spirit of Elisha	II Kings 2:9	And it came to pass, when they were gone over, that Elijah said unto Elisha, Ask what I shall do for thee, before I be taken away from thee. And Elisha said, I pray thee, let a double portion of thy spirit be upon me.

The Power Source of Elisha	II Kings 13:21	And it came to pass, as they were burying a man, that, behold, they cast the man into the sepulcher of Elisha: and when the man was let down, and touched the bones of Elisha, he revived, and stood up on his feet.
The Supplication of Hezekiah	II Kings 20:1-3	In those days was Hezekiah sick unto death. And the prophet Isaiah the son of Amoz came to him, and said unto him, Thus saith the LORD, Set thine house in order; for thou shalt die, and not live. I beseech thee, O LORD, remember now how I have walked before thee in truth and with a perfect heart, and have done that which is good in thy sight. And Hezekiah wept sore. Turn again, and tell Hezekiah the captain of my people, Thus saith the LORD, the God of David thy father, I have heard thy prayer, I have seen thy tears: behold, I will heal thee: on the third day thou shalt go up unto the house of the LORD.
The True Repentance and Reformation of King Josiah	II Kings 23:25	And like unto him was there no king before him, that turned to the lord with all his heart, and with all his soul, and with all his might, according to all the law of Moses; neither after him arose there any like him.
The Humility of a People Broken before God	II Chr 7:14	If my people who are called by my name, will humble themselves and pray and seek my face, then will I hear from heaven and I will forgive their sins and heal their land

The True Worship of Jehoshaphat	II Chr 20:18-22, 24	And Jehoshaphat bowed his head with his face to the ground: and all Judah and the inhabitants of Jerusalem fell before the LORD, worshipping the LORD. And the Levites, of the children of the Kohathites, and of the children of the Korhites, stood up to praise the LORD God of Israel with a loud voice on high. And they rose early in the morning, and went forth into the wilderness of Tekoa: and as they went forth, Jehoshaphat stood and said, Hear me, O Judah, and ye inhabitants of Jerusalem; Believe in the LORD your God, so shall ye be established; believe his prophets, so shall ye prosper. And when he had consulted with the people, he appointed singers unto the LORD, and that should praise the beauty of holiness, as they went out before the army, and to say, Praise the LORD; for his mercy endureth for ever. And when they began to sing and to praise, the LORD set ambushments against the children of Ammon, Moab, and mount Seir, which were come against Judah; and they were smitten. And when Judah came toward the watch tower in the wilderness, they looked unto the multitude, and, behold, they were dead bodies fallen to the earth, and none escaped.

The Servitude of Neziah	Ezra 1:3; 2:1, 54a	Who is there among you of all his people? his God be with him, and let him go up to Jerusalem, which is in Judah, and build the house of the LORD God of Israel, (he is the God,) which is in Jerusalem. Now these are the children of the province that went up out of the captivity, of those which had been carried away, whom Nebuchadnezzar the king of Babylon had carried away unto Babylon, and came again unto Jerusalem and Judah, every one unto his city; The children of Neziah
The Revival Ministry Ezra	Ezra 7:10	For Ezra had prepared his heart to seek the law of the LORD, and to do it, and to teach in Israel statutes and judgments.
The Fortitude Nehemiah	Neh 4:14,15	And I looked, and rose up, and said unto the nobles, and to the rulers, and to the rest of the people, Be not ye afraid of them: remember the Lord, which is great and terrible, and fight for your brethren, your sons, and your daughters, your wives, and your houses. And it came to pass, when our enemies heard that it was known unto us, and God had brought their counsel to nought, that we returned all of us to the wall, every one unto his work.
The Guidance/ Fortitude of Mordechai	Esth 4:14	For if thou altogether holdest thy peace at this time, then shall there enlargement and deliverance arise to the Jews from another place; but thou and they father's house shall be destroyed: and who knoweth whether thou art come to the kingdom for such a time as this?

The Conviction of Elihu (Job)	Job 32:21, 22	Let me not, I pray you, accept any man's person, neither let me give flattering titles unto man. For I know not to give flattering titles; in so doing my maker would soon take me away.
The Contrite Heart of Job	Job 42:3	Who is he that hideth counsel without knowledge? Therefore have I uttered that I understood not; things too wonderful for me, which I knew not.
The Restoration of Job	Job 42:10	And the Lord turned the captivity of Job, when he prayed for his friends: also the Lord gave twice as much as he had before.
The Priesthood of Melchizedek	Ps 110:4	The LORD hath sworn, and will not repent, Thou art a priest for ever after the order of Melchizedek.
The Lectures of King Lemuel	Prov 31:1	The words of king Lemuel, the prophecy that his mother taught him.
The Perspective of Isaiah	Isa 6:5	Then said I, Woe is me! For I am undone; because I am a man of unclean lips, and I dwell in the midst of a people of unclean lips: for mine eyes have seen the King, the Lord of hosts.
The Sensitivity of Jeremiah	Jer 4:19	My bowels, my bowels! I am pained at my very heart; my heart maketh a noise in me; I cannot hold my peace, because thou hast heard, O my soul, the sound of the trumpet, the alarm of war.
The Vision of Ezekiel	Ezek 40:2	In the visions of God brought he me into the land of Israel, and set me upon a very high mountain, by which was as the frame of a city on the south.

The Commitment of Daniel	Dan 1:8	But Daniel purposed in his heart that he would not defile himself with the portion of the king's meat, nor with the wine which he drank: therefore he requested of the prince of the eunuchs that he might not defile himself.
The Boldness of Hananiah, Azariah, and Meshielle	Dan 3:18	But if not, be it known unto thee, O king, that we will not serve thy gods, nor worship the golden image which thou hast set up.
The Unconditional Love of Hosea	Hos 3:1	Then said the Lord unto me, Go yet, love a woman beloved of her friend, yet an adulteress, according to the love of the Lord toward the children of Israel, who look to other gods, and love flagons of wine
The Sacrificial Heart of Malachi	Mal 3:8	Will a man rob God? Yet ye have robbed me. But ye say, wherein have we robbed thee? In tithes and offerings.
The Gospel of Matthew, Mark, Luke, and John	Matt 1:1; Mark 1:1; Luke 1:1-2; John 1:1	The book of the generation of Jesus Christ, the son of David, the son of Abraham. The beginning of the gospel of Jesus Christ, the Son of God. Forasmuch as many have taken in hand to set forth in order a declaration of those things which are most surely believed among us, Even as they delivered them unto us, which from the beginning were eyewitnesses, and ministers of the word; In the beginning was the Word, and the Word was with God, and the Word was God.
The Faith of the Centurion	Matt 8:8	The centurion answered and said, Lord, I am not worthy that thou shouldest come under my roof: but speak the word only, and my servant shall be healed.

The Ministry of Helps of Simon of Cyrene	Matt 27:32	And as they came out, they found a man of Cyrene, Simon by name: him they compelled to bear His cross.
The Righteousness of Zechariah	Luke 1:6	And they were both righteous before God, walking in all the commandments and ordinances of the Lord blameless
The Prophecy of Simeon	Luke 2:34	And Simeon blessed them, and said unto Mary his mother, Behold, this child is set for the fall and rising again of many in Israel: and for a sign which shall be spoken against.
The Strength of Peter	Acts 2:14	But Peter, standing up with the eleven, lifted up his voice, and said unto them, Ye men of Judea, and all ye that dwell at Jerusalem, be this known unto you, and hearken to my words:
The Vision of Stephen	Acts 7:55	But he, being full of the Holy Ghost, looked up steadfastly into heaven, and saw the glory of God, and Jesus standing on the right hand of God.
The Kingdom Building of Philip	Acts 8:35, 37, 38	Then Philip opened his mouth, and began at the same scripture, and preached unto him Jesus. And Philip said, if though believest with all thine heart, thou mayest. And he answered and said, I believe that Jesus Christ is the Son of God. And he commanded the chariot to stand still: and they went down both into the water, both Philip and the eunuch; and he baptized him.

The Anointing Power of Simeon (Niger) and Lucius of Cyrene	Acts 13:2-4	As they ministered to the lord, and fasted, the Holy Ghost said, separate me Barnabas and Saul for the work whereunto I have called then. And when they had fasted and prayed, and laid their hands on them, they sent them away. So they, being sent forth by the Holy Ghost, departed....
The Scholarship of Aquilla	Acts 18:26b	...whom when Aquilla and Priscilla had heard, they took him unto them, and expounded unto him the way of God more perfectly.
The Fearlessness of Paul	Acts 20:22-24	And now, behold, I go bound in the spirit unto Jerusalem, not knowing the things that shall befall me there: Save that the Holy Ghost witnesseth in every city, saying that bonds and afflictions abide me. But none of these things move me, neither count I my life dear unto myself, so that I might finish my course with joy, and the ministry, which I have received of the Lord Jesus, to testify the gospel of the grace of God.
The Sonship of Jesus	Gal 4:4,5	But when the fullness of the time was come, God sent forth his son, made of a woman, made under the law. To redeem them that were under law, that we might receive the adoption of sons.
The Commitment of Paul	Phil 3:14, 15	Brethren, I count not myself to have apprehended: but this one thing I do, forgetting those things which are behind, and reaching forth unto those things which are before, I press toward the mark for the prize of the high calling of God in Christ Jesus.

The Disposition of Timothy	I Tim 4:12	Let no man despise thy youth; but be thou an example of the believers, in word, in conversation, in charity, in spirit, in faith, in purity.
The Audacity of Onesiphorus	II Tim 1:16	The Lord give mercy unto the house of Onesiphorus; for he oft refreshed me, and was not ashamed of my chain:
The Preaching Ministry of Titus	Titus 1:5; 2:15	For this cause left I thee in Crete, that thou shouldest set in order the things that are wanting, and ordain elders in every city, as I had appointed thee: These things speak, and exhort, and rebuke with all authority. Let no man despise thee.
The Work Ethic of James	Jas 2:26	For as the body without the spirit is dead, so faith without works is dead also.
The Assurance of John 1, 2, 3	I John 5:13	These things have I written unto you that believe on the name of the Son of God; that ye may know that ye have eternal life, and that ye may believe on the name of the Son of God.
The Revelations of John	Rev 1:1, 2	The Revelation of Jesus Christ, which God gave unto him, to shew unto his servants things which must shortly come to pass; and he sent and signified it by his angel unto his servant John: Who bare record of the word of God, and of the testimony of Jesus Christ, and of all things that he saw.

PART 2

THE FRESH MEADOWS OF A GODLY PERSPECTIVE– IT'S REVELATION!

The series of compilations that follow contain revelations and reflections as given by God of a desire that we as His Christian Children should live more deliberately and excellently.

> *Arise, shine; for thy light is come, and the glory of the Lord is risen upon thee Isaiah 60:1*

> *We have also a more sure word of prophecy; whereunto ye do well that ye take heed, as unto a light that shineth in a dark place, until the day dawn, and the day star arise in your hearts: 2Peter 1:19*

Ever been in a meadow when the sun is the highest in the sky—at its brightest? Oh, how beautiful and refreshing the light of it. Everything sparkles and with every moment there is a glimpse or flicker of the light it has deposited.

Every tree leaf, every blade of grass, and every water droplet twinkles. In every eye, its brilliance is reflected beautifully. So bright has God called the shine of our lives for Him. By it and through us He lights the way and draws men out of darkness.

Revelation 12:11 tells us that they overcame him (Satan and his antics, devices and treachery) by the blood of the Lamb and by the Word of their testimony. As men come to belief in Christ, the sin that was attached is purified and rendered white and canceled by His life and by the source of His life (the blood that poured out). By it, He gives us new life.

Further, He is the Word; and when we speak, giving true testimony that points to Him, He is lifted up and He draws men. As did John when he wrote and testified revelations received on the Isle of Patmos, so too does our testimony bring salvation and hope to many. It draws their attention to the uplifted Christ; they look, and they live!

III

THE WIND OF YOUR DOCTRINE TAKES MY BREATH AWAY

In the meadow of Your Holiness
Are 'breath-taking' views

*Guide my steps, Dear Lord, and let me place my feet in your
footprints to walkout your Truths for the world to be drawn
By the power of your anointing upon me.*

BEHIND THE MATTER
"You have got to stop looking at the flesh–n–blood of a matter, and start looking to see the Spirit behind the matter."

Too often we get entangled in the who, what, and where factors of our experiences, giving reign to our carnal nature, rise to altercations, conflicts, and negative actions. Our reactions shamefully conform to the world's systems and standards. Conversely, God desires of us a determined heart to see Jesus in every circumstance so that our interactions are affected and driven by Him, alone. Even our thoughts have to line up with this Truth; and by it, the manipulation of the enemy is eradicated.

For we wrestle not against flesh–n–blood, but against principalities and powers and rulers of darkness and spiritual wickedness in high places (Ephesians 6:12). The flesh-n-blood of a matter is anything that blocks our view of God—the cares of this world, people (family, friends, enemies), self, other Christians. The Spirit of the matter is God's intent and purpose for us, or not, regarding the exchange.

Realizing that my thoughts even, especially, have to exceed this flesh and line up with God's Truth, I must stand casting down every vain imagination and high-minded thing that exalts itself above the knowledge of God [in me]. For so as he thinks, so is he. If born again, even my thoughts must be alive in spirit and dead to this flesh. The necessity of this is imperative to fulfilling a scripture very much akin to this: whatsoever things are pure, lovely, true, honest, just, and of good report; where there be any virtue or praise in it, may my thoughts fall there instead. Jesus is all these things and more. My resolve is to think on Him which satisfies all. Therefore, in the midst of my circumstances, I am empowered to set aside every weight that so easily besets me and run with patience the race that is set [by God] before me.

We are guilty of loss—the absence of Godly sight. Guilty, in so many instances, of getting caught up in the minors—jealously, gossip, misrepresentation, belligerence, color, gender, nationality, differences, traffic, hobbies, activities, events—which do not edify

God. We cover with the 'as long as it doesn't [physically] hurt anybody' syndrome. Eyes wide open my brothers and sisters, this is not a physical matter; it is a spiritual matter. We must take a true and honest look and be spiritually inclined to see the enemy at the root of our mess.

Even word-filled chain letters can come with the enemy attached. Unless we are 'spiritually' inclined and guarded against such, we will fail to see and miss it. Particularly, we seemingly miss it with the obvious ones and pass the contamination of the enemy along unaware. Several of them threaten punishment and demise if not forwarded. We must know such fear tactics are not of God and therefore should never be propagated by us.

Bootleg movies are another source of loss. This, I expect the world to misunderstand, not Christians. However, Christians are responding, "I didn't steal anything. I paid for this movie." Certainly, the FBI Warning regarding unauthorized sale of such items should be a red flag. In any case, even when specifically related scriptures are unknown, Christians should be tuned in to the Spirit witness that it is wrong. To purchase such is to buy into the flesh, into theft. The Word says "He who partners with a thief hates his own soul..." Proverbs 29:24. It is imperative that we *"come out from among them and touch not the unclean things."* II Corinthians 6:17

Some holidays and their celebration need to be examined for contamination, muddying by the enemy. Know that the celebration of darkness, evil, trickery, the list goes on and on, is not of God. Any idolatry, partying, or celebration of holidays where Jesus is not central, exclusively, is polluted by the enemy. **So much we miss that should not be!** We are charged to tune in and submit to God's Spirit to purge out the contamination.

When responding to the trials and challenges of circumstances even personal failures in my life, I do so with a truth that I have bought into and sell not for a lie. In truth, I have chosen God who first chose me and have resolved in my heart to give Him full control of all of me—my life, my future. Indeed, with Him in charge, nothing outside of His allowance can transpire in my life.

To make my position clear, the manifestation of my resolve is given. Simply, I know who my enemy is and that he stands at the root of it. Several years ago, feeling unjustly treated in the workplace by personnel with wrong and evil intentions, by Holy Spirit, Jesus raised in me this position. So, in direct opposition to the enemy's intention to keep those individuals in the path of eternal damnation and me in a place of heart devised to kill my witness, I refuse hate. I know who my enemy is. He is also their enemy.

In 'total' opposition to what the enemy sought to accomplish, I speak out. "Because you [Satan] had the audacity to send them into my space, invading my territory with your mess; and disturbing my peace, you must release. I call on the power of Almighty God to deliver them from your hands." Calling out to God each of them by name [JP, SH, DL, DS, DDM, DP, GM, JPF, TC, KM, TD, SE, FK, BC, EH, MN, and others], my fervent, sincere prayer became: *Lord, I thank You for shining the light of Your Truth on me and extending unto me Your delivering power.*

Recognizing that this salvation of mine is not for me alone, I continue to pray. *I pray that You, all knowing, perfectly able God, will bring them to realization of Your Truth and by that same Truth, their lies be clearly exposed. Expose 'til they are drawn in heart to acknowledge Your Truth and turn from unrighteousness, calling on the name of Jesus that they, too, might be saved.*

The Spirit behind the matter is this: They who are outside of Christ lose. I can only gain, regardless of the circumstances. Neither they nor the enemy who uses them is in charge. My father, the King, lays down the decrees, gives the orders, and makes the allowances for my life. He has assured me that by His authority all things work together for good to them who love Him and are the called according to His purpose.

He gives the oil of joy for mourning, beauty for ashes, abundance for sacrifice...my enemies to be my footstool.

The position of the 'Spirit' is far superior to the position of the 'flesh'. The flesh fosters hate and hankers demise, whereas the Spirit liberates and yields a peace that cannot be expressed. Simply, the devil is a liar and there is no truth in him. He is the father of lies. He is therefore incapable of anything other than producing and reproducing lies. The carnal mind is his playground, an enmity to our God. God deals in Spirit and Truth. In order to line up with God's Truth, we must first recognize our own flesh and reject it!

When we, Christians allow ourselves to be caught up in the flesh, the vain, carnal things of life, rather than the Spiritual, we make God and His Word a lie. The Spirit of the matter is this: It's not about me; It's about Him. Know that God has called us to lead the way to His righteousness, to set the example, to stand in the gap.

My fervent prayer has become: *"Lord, transform me. A renewed mind, I seek to be found in the likeness of my Savior. That...in seeing, I might see through the eyes of Jesus; in hearing, I might listen with the ears of the Son; in interacting with others, I may do so with the compassionate heart of the Lamb; in living, I may live the Truth of the Son. In absolute obedience and trust, I submit that the will of God may be done in me as it is in Heaven—without apprehension and without delay. That I be sober; that I be vigilant first and foremost against the operation of this [my own] flesh!*

What's in your heart? Take a good look. Be honest. Accept what Holy Spirit shows you. Then, for all unrighteousness, 'testify against it'. Call out those things and God will pluck them out one by one.

WWJD (*What would Jesus Do?*) is a simple yet profound concept.

WHO WILL?

"I will do and who will let it!"

Indeed, a profound statement for **there is none that can challenge my God**. Convinced for some years that its source was the Bible, I unsuccessfully sought a scriptural reference for the statement which manifested during a study of Moses. It was the early stages of the Exodus about Moses' request of God to show him His glory. As He covered Moses' eyes and passed by allowing Moses to see only His backside, God spoke regarding Himself, "The Lord, The Lord God, merciful and gracious, longsuffering, and abundant in goodness and truth, keeping mercy for thousands, forgiving iniquity and transgression and sin..." Exodus 34:6,7a.

Having quoted "I will do and who will let it!" many times, I exhaustively searched both electronically and manually but could not find the exact quote in scripture. I vividly remember inquiring of God what He meant by this and His answer to my question. The following briefly conveys the totality of His response.

He is right in all His ways. There is none that dares to question Him. There are no checks-and-balances. There is none that can qualify to oversee Him. "I answer to none and from none do I seek permission," saith the Master. He defines it. He alone sets the standard. He is God the authority, the majority, the verdict, the bottom line, the final say in all matters!

May your meditations on this leave you with the understanding, or refreshing, that **God sets the standard**; and we are to walk in that standard. Anyone who attempts to come to God, to claim God, apart from this standard is but a thief and a robber. He has established the order of the natural. No matter what man adds, perpetrates, or accepts as standard, inclusive, or fair, the bottom line begins and ends with the points on God's vector, exclusively. How dare we try to reorder or accept the reorder of what Sovereign God has already ordered. That's OUT OF ORDER.

Most recently, during the final phases of editing this book, another search for a scriptural reference commenced. Coming across at last, the scripture, Isaiah 43:13, spotlighted. Praise God!

GET IT RIGHT

"The salvation of a lot of individuals is dependent on you getting it right, [your name]"

God blew my mind with this one. I was struggling with compromise and letting advocates of the enemy into my space. Things and individuals unlike my God attached themselves to me. This shameful period brought much grief to the Spirit of my God. On two occasions He spoke the above to me, personally addressing me by name. Sweetly, gently, yet firmly He stepped each time speaking to my heart's ear, these exact words, then left. However, His words never left me and remain resonant in my ear.

For when for the time ye ought to be teachers, ye have need that one teach you again which be the first principles of the oracles of God; and are become such as have need of milk, and not of strong meat. Hebrew 5:12

We, children of the Most-High, are called to a position of:
_ No compromise
_ Setting the standard

The standard is Jesus. My Jesus humbled himself in obedience unto death. This he did not for himself for he was already royalty. He did it for you and me. Without it, we would not have realized the hope of salvation.

God caused me to recognize it this way: Once I accepted Jesus Christ as my Lord and Savior, in that instance I was saved, received Holy Spirit and my status with God changed. This earth was no longer my home. I became a sojourner to this earth and Heaven became my destination. As a sojourner, my purpose is to lay down roots and to lay down truths where defined and assigned to me by my Father, the King.

Heaven is my home. It is settled for me. My inheritance is sure. However, at a place of God's understanding, I realize that "this thing is not about me". My being here is about God, to affect in righteousness and to strengthen in weakness those He attaches to me during this earthly sojourn. It's about kingdom building and everything He purposes for it through my living witness.

Through salvation, my purpose has become "kingdom building". It is to walk in maturity and build the walls of my Father's kingdom while tearing down the walls of the enemy's kingdom—one saved, sanctified, and empowered soul at a time.

Let him know, that he which converteth the sinner from the error of his way shall save a soul from death, and shall hide a multitude of sins. James 5:20

My prayer became: **As it was with my Savior, I would that I not lose a one that You have given me to affect unto righteousness; that You would protect and preserve them unto the day of their deliverance.**

NO EXCUSE

"Those with access to the Truth have no excuse operating in anything other than that Truth."

Our Father is speaking of those saved, with Holy Spirit residing inside. Therein is our access to the Truth, Jesus Christ. Jesus said of Holy Spirit, 'He shall lead and guide you to all Truth. That which He hears [from Me] will He speak unto you'.

Jesus is the way, truth, and life to which Holy Spirit gives us witness. We have direct access to God's answers and directions. Simply, it is a matter of us acting on those truths rather than choosing our own way. God is interested in what we do, even the most minute details—attitudes, thoughts, physical expressions.

We have been equipped with everything we need. The power lives in us; we need only to live it.

There is 'no excuse' for actions other than those that exemplify Jesus in us. So, if we find ourselves acting outside of the Truth, let us withdraw quickly and repent to God. Even apologize to those affected by our ungodly behavior. Such renouncements render the enemy powerless to stand accusing our God through us.

Holy Spirit gave me these words to pray regarding my hiccups: **"Lord, let no fruit come of it for the enemy."**

Read also, *The Standard*, in the Breath of Life section of this book.

IMPRESS ME

"Every interface is an opportunity to impress Me on somebody."

Whether in verse, in deed, or in living example, the light and love of Jesus should shine through all that we do. We are children of the King and the peculiarity of our royal status should stand out from what is common. Royalty distinguish themselves in posture, conversation, attire, places ventured, and company kept, ever careful not to shame the King.

Once I accepted in my heart and spoke Jesus Christ as Lord and Savior, the enemy, bound by the terms of the ransom Jesus had already paid, had to let me go. The enemy knows that I am now sealed and cannot be snatched from my Savior's hand. The enemy, a thief and a liar, predatorily seeks to devour. He is determined and relentless, in his quest to rob, kill, and destroy—not my physical body—my witness. I, therefore, am compelled to stand armored in God's righteousness. Thanks to my God for the indwelling of Holy Spirit who guides me to walk in His statutes and to keep His ways.

A heart that delights in God...*Let your light so shine before men, that they may see your good works, and glorify your Father which is in heaven.* Matthew 5:16

Our lifestyle, our interfaces, our actions...all that we do and all that we attach ourselves to should be a glowing reflection of Truth lighting the way to our God. Let us consider our every action, to live a life that lifts up Jesus, to draw all to Him.

SAVED?

"There are many who think they are saved, when they are not."

These are exactly the words of the Master to my heart concerning the "once saved, always saved" concept. That concept has made us a bit too comfortable with the operation of this flesh. Don't get me wrong, I agree wholeheartedly that none can snatch us out of His hand. My concern was with what I had observed taking place in the hearts of people that I knew, especially family members. Though none could take them out of Jesus' hand, it appears that one certainly can make a choice to denounce God. Thus, one can walk out of promise and denounce their salvation, I believe.

I saw individuals baptized, accepting Jesus as Savior, and reared in churches where the same salvation that they claim was promoted as occurring only through Jesus. Yet, my heart fails me. Some individuals have denounced and currently question His existence or simply express a belief that He doesn't exist at all. They have yoked themselves up with atheists; they claim the new world view that they are empowered to be their own gods; they have chosen and adopted beliefs of religious denominations that reject Jesus as the Son of God.

Other baptized individuals who apparently accepted Jesus Christ as Savior, though they have not walked away from Jesus-based denominations, have taken on positions of belief that are anti-God. They have bought into the lie that there are other ways to God besides Jesus. They espouse that works and what good you do for others are what get you into Heaven. In every adversity that comes their way, they excuse themselves to respond like the world, without any Godly restraint and justify their actions with 'God knows my heart'. As if that makes the wrong alright with God, they further those discussions with 'When it's time for me to change, God will let me know' and may add 'When God comes and tells me to change it; then I'll believe it' or 'until God shows it to me, I am not changing.'

Deeming, somehow, that others who are speaking to them, even quoting scripture, don't qualify. Further, the same individuals taking these positions are the same ones who do not actively nor personally study God's word; their attendance at Sunday School and Bible Studies is practically non-existent. For this reason, they keep missing it and remain without Spiritual growth. Thus, the flesh keeps overruling the Spirit. Too busy for Bible Study and sometimes church but will shut everything down to avoid missing a ball game. The door is closed to any appeal to do things differently or to embrace God's truths; and there is no apparent witness of the Spirit in them to the Truth that God is sending their way.

There is a new-age excuse: 'Not everybody is where you are.' 'Not everybody wants what you want.' 'People don't want all that.' 'It doesn't take all that.' Exasperating, though it is, I simply prod, "Give me one good reason why not. Why wouldn't anyone want this?" In situations where Truth comes but there is no witness in us that it is indeed Truth, when we reject anything that means we must change something, or when things born outside of Truth become common ground and find a place of acceptance in a person's heart, God says, **"The foundation of their salvation is in question or at the least, their witness has been contaminated."**

Pondering this thing, I cried out to God, "How is the world going to get any better, if the church doesn't aspire to do better?" Intense is my frustration regarding the matter of us calling ourselves Christian, yet setting boundaries on God in rejection of His Truths. By far the most dangerous, I believe, is the promotion in conversation, in action, and in thought things that are not of God's heart. With our contaminated, polluted, perhaps dead witness, we become voices for the enemy.

From these thoughts, I dialogued, "Father, is it that, though none can snatch us from Your hands, we can actually reject our salvation?" Recapitulation of God's response follows. 'All that aside, whether people can receive that as a possibility or not, what **it really comes down to is the question of whether they are saved in the first place.** For there are

many who think they are saved but they are not. They have deceived themselves and in essence, have been deceived by the church. They think that their baptism ceremony established their salvation. Many think that repeating the words of the sinner's prayer took care of it. Many are even more confused in that they have

forgotten whether they were baptized or even accepted my Son but assume they must be saved considering they have been in the church all their lives and have many good deeds to support it.'

The Word of God expressly states: *That if thou shalt confess with thy mouth the Lord Jesus* **and believe in thine heart** *that God hath raised Him from the dead, thou shalt be saved. For with the heart man believeth unto righteousness; and with the mouth confession is made unto salvation.* (Romans 10:9-10) A related scripture is: *Out of the mouth proceed the issues of the heart.* (Matt 15:18)

As defined in the scriptures, I received this from God in those moments of reflection. God is the only discerner of the thoughts and intents of the heart. Heart witness is unquestionably confirmed by personal vocalization, communication from an individual's mouth of their own language, vocabulary, and means. "In order to affirmatively receive My Son, **they must open their mouths and speak what is in their own hearts, not yours**", saith the Lord. With no heart witness, vocalization is merely recitation, rhetoric. It has become so common ground in our churches to do mass salvation—'repeat after me' —giving a place for some to hide without open confession. I believe we are often missing this truth and therefore in danger of causing some individuals to miss true salvation. Therefore this process must be approached with extreme caution and clarity. Be careful that it is not a 'going through the motions', 'getting the numbers' event.

The way to the sheep is Jesus. He who comes up any other way is a thief and a robber. You know the fate of a thief, right? Luke 11:28, implores us to *'Let a man examine, himself....'* A similar scripture is: *Let a man be careful that he think he stand, lest he fall.* (I Corinthians 10:12) God has called us to examine ourselves. Consider Jesus' statements in Matthew 7:20-23 and in the Parable of the Wedding Feast, Matthew 22:1-14. Let us not only consider those statements but measure ourselves against them.

When those who were initially invited to the wedding feast failed to make an appearance, Jesus sent His servants, evangelists, missionaries, ministers, etc., into the highways and by-ways to extend an invitation to those hearts sincerely desiring Truth yet not knowing where to find it. The hungry, the empty, the thirsty, they came. However, among the guest at the feast, one was found without the proper wedding garment. The individual was not covered in the blood of Jesus. Jesus died on that cross, our propitiation. His blood freely shed and freely given for the covering required to enter into the Master's rest—the wedding garment necessary to partake of the feast.

Biblical history holds that the master of the house furnished wedding apparel for guest to don before entering the feast. Freely given so that all a guest had to do was accept it and put it on. Consider the one guest found without a garment. That guest preferred the clothes that he or she was wearing, and, therefore, simply refused to wear the wedding garment.

Some individuals, indeed misguided, think they earn a right to heaven just by going to church and doing the works. God's response is this, *'Yeah, you accepted, at least recited verbally, that Jesus is the Son of God; yet, it was not in the heart.'* Perhaps it was an act born out of the excitement of the moment. It felt good. The atmosphere was just right. Everyone else was doing it. Perhaps you thought it made sense since you had been going to church for years anyway. An accident or sickness spooked you into trying to cover self. God says, *'But, you never put on the wedding garment because it was not in the heart. **In your heart** you didn't believe, you didn't receive it so you were never covered in the garment of My Son's blood.'*

The Lord avows, *'You entered My feast without the proper garment. You entered with your own filthy rags. Did you not realize that you were going to stand out with your black on among all those in white apparel? Indeed, a tree is known by the fruit it bears. Behold, things with you are old when all should have become new. You stand out and it is clear that you don't belong at My feast. Get out and be thrown into everlasting fire where there will be wailing and gnashing of teeth.'* Further, the Lord declares, *'I tell you many will come to Me in that day with their black on, claiming how they cast out demons, prophesied in My name. I will respond, 'you don't have the proper garment on. You are not covered in my blood. There is therefore no way that you know Me, nor I you!'*

Contemplate 1 Samuel 4:3-10. The children of Israel, in all their idolatries, thought themselves safe. After all, Abraham was their Father and the Ark of the Covenant to them was a covering. Unfortunately, they neither understood nor revered God as the source. And so were oblivious when the presence of the Lord left them. Ultimately, they were delivered into the hands of the enemy. Much like the Israelites, some individuals nowadays are too comfortable with the world and have rested their hopes and security in the wrong things. They think that blood family, church affiliation, money, deeds, and all things worldly define their right to the blessings of God. The Spirit of Almighty God dwells not in an unclean temple. (For more, read 2 Chronicles 36:15-21)

What fruit are you bearing that release the anointing, power, and glory of the Master? Or is it simply the flesh that's getting the gratification?

In this, I recall watching a Christian broadcast as a long-time evangelist and pastor shared his testimony. He had spent decades in the ministry, believing and operating in a works-based life. In time, God began to pull and tug on his heart. Periodically, the question of his salvation would rise up in him, but he would override it, count his works, and satisfied, decide that he was okay. But, in time, glory to God, he came face-to-face with the Truth of the condition of his life. He was not saved and headed for this exact confrontation with Jesus. He submitted to that Truth and received his salvation.

May God expose to every heart that is out of order, the Truth of it. This is heavy, but like my Savior, I would that ALL come into the acknowledgment of the Truth and turn from unrighteousness so that no man perishes.

Simply, I pray: **My God! Don't let us miss You!**

<u>Study also:</u>

Matthew 8:11, 12	Hebrews 10:38, 39
Luke 13:24-28	I John 2:16-19
I Corinthians 11:28	

SET UP

"I set the enemy up to give you a victory."

Thinking on this, I'm reminded of an old song with these profound words:

> *Heir of salvation; purchased by God*
> *Born of His Spirit; washed in His blood*
> ...
> *Oh, what a foretaste of Glory divine.*

Whether we catch it or not, even in the midst of our adversities, God provides us a peek into what He has in store. Working over twenty years for two employers, one for 18 ½ years and the other for 2, I experienced various modes of adversity. Yet, during the greatest periods of adversity that targeted me, I saw God. Often overruling their ill intentions, God allowed me a foretaste of His authority.

One occurrence was during the restart of chemical operations from a planned outage. As I confirmed and reset many computer control settings, a particular one eluded me. Adjustments were made in a couple places; and, aware that one other setting needed adjustment, I went to the precise spot for the code change. However, when I double-checked, as was my standard approach, the identity of the code read something entirely different. After completing my efforts, I left instructions with operators for restarting operations then went home still perplexed about that code but confident that safeguards imbedded into the control system would prevent any potential issues associated with this minor concern. That is, failing to consider that one of the operators would override the safeguard and create issues.

Bottom line, early the next morning, I got a call at home. While I worked to identify the corrections needed for resolution, a concerted effort from the other end in determined opposition of me, met me with hostility as they refused to interface with me. Already, at the foreman's request, an engineer from another facility had spent several hours assisting them to no avail. The enemy so opposed me that my mind confounded the resolution.

Arriving at the facility mid-morning, I trended the data showing the performance issues and formulated a resolution for a diagnosis that, unbeknownst to me, was off. I typed an email explaining the intended resolution to the problem; but strangely, I felt constrained and could not yet send it. Getting up from my desk to take a walk; I motioned to the door and felt an even greater restraint as I flopped back down in my chair. Instantly, my eyes fell on the answer. Immediately, I checked and adjusted the same data that I had looked for the day before. Checking the exact location, there in crystal clear clarity was what I could not see previously. The problem was eliminated. I amended the email to reflect my findings, sent it to distribution, and left.

While walking the 12-minute hike to my car, I praised God for how He had blinded their eyes to the 'simple' answer and covered me. Though, I felt compelled to ask, "Why didn't You allow me to see the data when I looked for it yesterday?" Had I found and adjusted the data then, it would have served as an additional preventive from the upset condition caused by the operator. My God quickly responded and with a voice of triumph he said, "I set the enemy up to give you a victory!" Wow! That's all I could articulate. Wow.

Another notable experience occurred during my second employment. There, unfounded opposition surfaced and drove the false accusation that I had conflict with another engineer. Regarding that claim, the typical stereotypes where written into my performance evaluation. Of all my adversarial work experiences, that at my second facility of employment was the most frustrating. God would not allow me to speak my defense or challenge management as I had done in the past. The only option was to totally trust Him. It was a time of growth and a new level that God was taking me to.

In short, the end of the matter is this: At the point that they put in writing this false claim with which they purposed in their hearts my demise, my God rose to my defense. Within two months, a situation arose which forced them to terminate that individual. When God revealed the truth of what He had prevailed for me, when it finally hit my radar screen months later, I was floored. He said, "Foretaste, just a foretaste of My Glory divine."

Later reflecting on it, He reminded me that the Pharisees at one point had purposed to stone Jesus and how He walked on through them, untouched. Untouched because, according to the word, "His time was not yet." Likewise, it was not yet the appointed time for me to be crucified, thus my God said, "Not so", and it was not so. Amazed, I humbly responded, **"Lord, God, who am I that You are mindful of lowly me? Oh, God, You are so awesome! I would but that I not fail You; be Thou my help and my strength and prevail over my weaknesses. My desire is Your pleasure, all my days."**

You see? God does not need a 'perfect person'. He simply desires and makes use of, and is poised to prevail on behalf of a person with a 'perfect heart'. God says, I want you to know the extent to which I am able to cover you. Know that I am indeed, exclusively in charge of your destiny and they cannot touch you without My allowance. The enemy can do nothing before the appointed time.

With His great covering, God simply gives us, **"a foretaste of His Glory, divine!"**

Revelation reminds me that this Glory we taste of right now will shine so bright in the coming kingdom that there will be no need for the sun. That Glory where Truth and Righteousness will reside and prevail in a power that, though the doors of the Kingdom remain open at all times, gives no cause for alarm or concern because nothing unlike Jesus can enter in.

Even while we are yet on this earth, our lives can and should touch that truth.

BURIED DEAD OR ALIVE?

"It's a dangerous thing to keep digging up that which I [God] have buried."

Forgetting those things which are behind and looking forward unto those things which are before; I press toward the mark of the high call of God which is in Christ Jesus... Philippians 3:14

The enemy will attempt to discourage even shame you to silence. If that fails, he will attempt to pull up your past in an effort to close another person's ear to you. Be encouraged, God says, "All that he will pull up is you clean, pure, and washed in the blood of My Son."

For several years after God's merciful deliverance of me from my situation of sin and shame (Section III, *"It's My Fault"*), each time I reflected on my wretchedness, I would cry and repent repetitively to God for my gross failure. Having come to the place where God wants all of us, I loathed this flesh and all that it had operated in against my God's righteousness. Despite my deliverance from that bondage of compromise, I continually, rehashed my repentance, sobbing, for so greatly missing the mark and failing those who truly needed to see God's light. God allowed it to go on and just listened for about four years. Finally, He responded, speaking firmly and intently to me, "Gwen. Gwen! I don't remember. I really don't remember." Since that day, I have not repeated that request for forgiveness. God, through His Spirit, made it clear that it was buried by Him. Any attempt of the enemy to dig it up again will only reveal things perfect, righteous, and good.

God gave it to me to speak this every time the enemy stirred thoughts of guilt and shame: "The blood of Jesus has cleansed me and anything you attempt to bring up regarding me, according to the Word of God shall be white as snow." In tandem, there is a word that was given for the enemy's advocates, those who allow themselves to be used, those who endeavor to keep past failures in front of others. "It's a dangerous thing to keep trying to dig up that which God has buried." Take confidence that God's hand is against all who, as advocates of the enemy, try to hold it over you and to keep it in front of you.

Be affirmed that in 'true, heart' repentance, God, by the blood of Jesus, cancels all debt. It is gone! There is reconciliation and restoration beyond our failures, our sins, backsliding, etc. Sweet release from the past so that we can now move forward to what is ahead. What's ahead? Ahead are the tools of empowerment to be victorious in our individual ministries, especially the ministry of *'how we live'* before men.

My past, present, and future sins; all covered by the blood...well penned words from a song of which I am reminded. Do not let the enemy keep pushing your head down in a slump over your past. A point of encouragement for which I am so grateful to have heard is: 'When the devil reminds you of your past, you remind him of his future.'

Humble your hearts, sons of God, but lift your heads. Look up! For your liberty is above and not below; in front of you and not behind.

Stand fast, therefore in the liberty wherewith Christ has made us free; and be not entangled again with the yoke of bondage. Galatians 5:1

IV

YOU ARE THE BREATH OF LIFE, THE QUICKENING WORD, ALIVE IN ME

In the meadow of Your Holiness are
'living' views

*Guide my meditations, Dear Lord. Reveal Your heart to me and
let me uncover Your Righteousness for the world.
Mature me, Oh Lord, so that I can be enlightened
by the counsel of your perfect wisdom.*

RESURRECTION

Again, mentally sifting through the promises of my God, I reflect on His set up of the enemy just to show Himself mighty on my behalf, giving me victory...

Thinking on my experiences, my mediations led to the Savior. I considered how, though He escaped their devices many times, eventually, they did succeed in killing Him. I contemplated one specific escape. The events of Jesus' miraculous escape from attempts to stone Him played in my head. I considered the difference. The intent to stone Him could not succeed because it was neither assigned by the Master as the appointed time nor the appointed method of death. It could only be accomplished to God's glory, fulfilling the scriptures by way of the cross. God softly interjected, "Resurrection".

My thoughts processed to a place of thanksgiving as I took into account the great sacrifice God made, how my many sins were laid on Him, and all that He endured for me. I set my affections on the cross expressing, "Thank You for the cross." As those thoughts ceased, there was a pause then God declared resoundingly, "But He rose, Gwen! He rose! He rose!" In that moment it became clear—the ultimate hope is not in the cross alone, but founded securely in the power of the resurrection.

At the appointed time of His deliverance, God released the enemy to take my Savior's life. Oh, but Glory Hallelujah! Though my Savior's body lay in a dark damp cave for 3 days, with death He took into that grave all past, present, and future sins. While there, He eliminated sin's power, conquered the darkness, and rose up with ALL power in His hands. Further, by His obedience, at His resurrection came His dominion, even the dominion of His name, over all things. Even the devil is subject to it. The enemy is constrained to obey all that comes by the name Jesus, including our release from the bondage of sin.

My brothers and my sisters, God says, don't get bogged down with how ugly, unfair, evil it looks; nor how painful it feels or how guilty you may appear when you are crucified. You see? Satan thinks he has the upper hand. He thinks he can kill your spirit. He thinks you're

sure to give up. He thinks that he is controlling your outcome and that he can make it permanent. He is determined in His ultimate goal, to kill your witness and cost many the Kingdom.

"Not so." saith the Lord. "Know that 'I set the enemy up to give you a victory'. Out of your endurance, obedience, faithful trust, and bold stance for My Truths, I have prepared the windows of heaven to pour out on you a blessing that will flow beyond you to the multitudes. There is an anointing in the overflow to come, that the enemy cannot stop. There is salvation and deliverance of a multitude stored up in your testimony. For I am the Author and the Finisher of your faith and to your adversities, there is not only an expected end but a coming resurrection power that cannot be contained nor constrained."

Just ask Joseph or Job; or simply consider David. I have no doubt Peter and Paul would have much to say regarding this matter. In fact, it can be summed up in Paul's words:

II Corinthians 4: 9,10...*Persecuted, but not forsaken; cast down, but not destroyed; Always bearing about in the body the dying of the Lord Jesus, that the life also of Jesus might be made manifest in our body.*

The Glory is in the Resurrection!

I declare to the enemy, and before my God: "My victory is sure and my resurrection is certain!"

THE ULTIMATE RESTORATION

That man return to his original state or position with God, **the fellowship and dominion of Adam before the fall,** is the ultimate restoration!

Genesis 1:26-31 [The Edenic Covenant] set man at a place of dominance over all living creatures and things upon the face of the earth. There was no sickness. There was no disease. Hearts were pure, and innocence prevailed. It didn't even rain. Adam physically walked and talked with God. God insured man's every provision, so he lacked nothing.

In one of many meditations on **Galatians 5:1**, I heard the Spirit say, "True liberty is that which Adam walked in before the fall." Supported by both **Romans (12:1, 2)** and **Joshua (1:7b, 8)**, free is a renewed mind and body functioning as the living sacrifice called by God. That person not only has a right but a charge to walk in that freedom, Adamic freedom—free from sickness/disease, free from endangerment of animals, at one, personal and intimate, with God.

Through the power of Jesus' blood and the power of His name, we have been restored to go in and retake possession of the land of plenty in every aspect of our lives—spiritually, mentally, physically, and economically. Spoken first to Abraham (**Genesis 13:14-17**) and later reiterated to Joshua (Joshua 1:1-11), God said, *Every place that the sole of your foot shall tread upon, that have I given unto you,… go in to possess the land which the Lord your God giveth you to possess it.*

God desires us to tap into the power of access that is fully achievable in Him. Just as it was made available to Adam who physically had the power and presence of God with him at all times. God has given and restored us to a place of access to the same. His Spirit reveals that as the chosen of God, we can walk in spiritual authority over all that goes on in the atmosphere around us and over the environments God has assigned us to. In the workplace, at home and over the land on which it resides, the house of worship where He has called us to establish our membership, wherever our feet shall tread, we have access to God's authority to cause even the atmosphere to line up with His Truth.

The way I received it is that **at my entrance to a place, it's me and the Majority. This body is a temple of God's Holy Spirit. He dwells here; therefore, anything unlike Him cannot stand in His presence. All must either line up with Truth or submit to His authority and flee.**

Yes, I am more than a conqueror through Christ which strengthens me.

We must yield as Ezekiel (6:1-7) to the Lord's instruction and prophesy against the mountains. "And say, *Ye mountains of Israel, hear the word of the Lord God; Thus saith the Lord God to the mountains, to the hills, to the rivers, and to the valleys; Behold, I, even I, will bring a sword upon you and I will destroy your high places.*" In us, the sword is the Spirit. In us, God will bring low everything that attempts to exalt itself above the knowledge and authority of the Almighty.

Further, **Isaiah (40:4, 5)** lends us confidence and hope through the assurance that not only will the exalted be brought low (downcast) but the down-trodden, the oppressed, the afflicted—the humble in righteousness—shall be exalted. It is my contention that in us the power of God is there to tap into this, even now. The blood of Jesus has qualified it; His resurrection has endowed it; and His mouth has spoken it through **Luke (10:19)**.

The ultimate restoration will be completed and sealed with the coming of the new earth and kingdom of our King. **Revelations (7:17; 21:4-7; 21:22-27), Isaiah (25:8), I Corinthians (15:54),** and **I John (3:2)** give a hope of glory that we can take confidence in. All will be set in order with all influence of evil eradicated. No medicine, no locks, no alarms, no guards, no weapons will be necessary as the power of the glory of the Almighty shines its full brilliance in the New Jerusalem. Know that nothing unlike Him will enter.

I'm convinced that we shall find exceedingly more than the first Adam enjoyed, for eyes have not seen, nor ears heard, nor has it entered into the heart of man what God has in store.

Hallelujah!

IT IS ALREADY DONE

And I will give unto thee the keys of the kingdom of Heaven: and whatsoever thou shalt bind on earth shall be bound in Heaven: and whatsoever thou shalt loose on earth shall be loosed in Heaven. (Matthew 16:19)

When ministering to my spirit regarding this scripture, God spoke, "In Heaven, it's already done. Whatsoever you bind in earth IS bound in heaven; and whatsoever you loose on earth IS loosed in heaven."

With Jesus, in Jesus, you cannot lose. Know that your victory is sure. It was secured a long time ago. At the very moment that Satan was banished from heaven, victory was secured; the authority of heaven sealed, irreversible.

Jesus further sealed the matter when He went down into that grave, and with that conquered both death and hell. He rose and ascended into the clouds with all power in heaven and in the earth. Giving Him a name that is above any other name, God secured it. *'That at the name Jesus every knee shall bow of things in heaven, and things in earth, and things under the earth; and every tongue shall confess that Jesus Christ is Lord...'* Even the enemy is subject to the authority of Heaven's Son. Through His Word (Luke 10:19), He has imparted that power unto us.

The assurance of hope from which comes our endurance is that **Heaven has already settled the matter**. Our victory is sure; the promises of God are solid. The only thing that stands between us and those promises is time. Simply, on this earth, we must get to the place and time to receive what Heaven has already done! When we come to a point of believing God, expectantly; and further, when we speak it and finally agree with Heaven in our hearts, we affect victory's release. It shall be done (for me) as in Heaven.

"IT'S MY FAULT"

In the midst of a divorce after 18 years, 8 courted by and 10 married to the same individual, I found myself thrown, sink or swim, into the singles arena. Foolishly leaning on my own understanding, I allowed the enemy substantial access and began dwelling on the flesh's version of the matter. My self-focus, pity party was about all that I had tried to do right and all the wrong that had come through my ex. As well, earthly things lost or unattained because of it.

For reasons unknown but certainly out of self-righteousness and a fool's heart, I completely overlooked how close I had grown in spirit to God. A relationship I had come to rely on. Drawn to a place in His presence where so clearly his voice I heard. I lost focus on the power of God's grace and favor all around me: my two beautiful girls who were produced and birthed in holiness, friends who were Godly, strong women of the Word, and more.

During the time spent in a fool's arena, the enemy infiltrated. His advocates were primed to affect my life and kill my witness. Blindsided, I was unprepared and missed the onslaught. While driving my husband's repetitive failures and heart away from me, the enemy was also setting his advocates' sight on me. Drawn by the challenge, breaking me was the ultimate prize.

What's more, while married and comfortable with that commitment, I naively allowed myself to be befriended by one of those advocates who I knew was non-Christian and was shameless in his unrighteousness. Dissolution of my marriage quickly wrought a battlefield of the mind in which the enemy waged war on me that ensued immediately. Letting in the first selfish thought accelerated sin's infestation to a point beyond which I had the strength to overcome.

Much worse, while going through the crisis in my marriage that inevitably led me to leave my husband, I foolishly leaned on that non-Christian friend rather than on a Godly friend. For me, separated with divorce imminent and all that followed was a miserable time that I wouldn't wish on an enemy. He, as well as another of the enemy's advocates, operated a game of manipulation targeting me and attempting to destroy my hope, my values, my reputation—my witness. Born of nothing but a heart of hatred, the advocates featured in the compromise of my heart's commitment to never again engage in sex apart from marriage.

Though all seemed lost, really **nothing was**. So glad to know that God, not man, has the final say. In short, merciful God processed me through my mess 'til He brought me out on the other side. He restored me and positioned me to look back on my mess, not as Lot's wife longing to return to it, but out of His Spirit of deliverance, knowing that, this time, I would never enter that mess again.

As I continued to grow back to that close relationship with God over the following years, reflections of this experience would come to me and new revelations for a singles ministry would come out of it. Early in this process of periodic reflection, I was brought to a place of looking at all the pain, anguish, and shame in perspective of the good that Faithful God was working out of my mess. At my request, the Spirit arrested my heart in this matter so that now my reflections are only from "righteous" perspectives. Inevitably came my point of awesome truth regarding the evil that had been so relentlessly and deliberately perpetrated against me—**"It's my fault."**

A simple matter of Truth, the advocates perpetrating the games that affected my operation of compromise were doing the only things they knew to do. They had long given their lives and practice over to filthy and lascivious living. It was what they knew. I, however, failed to operate in what I knew. I was the one with the Truth living in me. I was the one with the charge of righteousness. There was a way of escape. I simply failed to take it. As a result, I grieved God's sweet Holy Spirit. By my actions, not theirs, my witness became contaminated. By not living righteously before them, I failed to show them that, though challenging, it is possible.

Humbly, I am convinced that before any healing can begin, past wrongs must be owned; and healing has to come before the full impact of our ministry, current and future, can effectively reach the summit that God intends. Lord, *"against Thee only have I sinned and done this evil in Thy sight"*. (David's Psalm) The shame that comes with acknowledgement and ownership of unrighteousness is a good place to be but not to stay. By the enemy's design, the spirit of shame keeps us stagnant, causing us to curl up and wallow in depression. But God says, "Not so."

At this point of my struggle in the singles arena, I found in my heart, a deep indebtedness to God. He was merciful beyond measure. Instead of leaving me in my mess, He kept His hand on me. Most certainly, with His right hand, He upheld me.

Like never before, I began to pray in earnest hope of salvation for the enemy's advocates. Revelation of fault, as given by Holy Spirit, refreshed in me that this was not a flesh-n-blood wrestle. It was a direct act and operation of the enemy of God against my witness. The enemy determined to delay, utterly contaminate, and destroy, if possible, my witness. For all that had transpired, I turned my hatred to the real enemies—Satan and this flesh. While calling on and claiming the empowerment of the Spirit to override it, I began to speak death to this flesh. In answer to Satan, I prayed redemption and restoration— that God would redeem my failure through salvation of the enemy's advocates; praying He would give them another witness and draw their hearts to Him.

Ultimately, in my struggle, there was no other choice except to totally surrender it to God. To my Master, I expressed, "Lord, I don't trust this flesh. It is incapable of getting this right. I resolve to separate myself from and from myself the right hand and the eye that so offends your Spirit in me. I resolve in my heart that You are more than enough. You exceed the necessary. For the rest of my days, only You, Jesus, is a great place to be!" When I finally took this position against my constant failures, God moved. Satisfied in the Truth, the bottom line for my life is that God is more than enough for the rest of my days.

Out of this shame come declarations that the operations of judgment, arrogance and self-righteousness never live to rule in me and that humility ever be my banner. I am a wretch, indeed, without Him. For there is no good thing going on in this flesh, but God!

Forgetting those things which are behind and looking toward those things which are before, I press toward the mark. Indeed, **if those things left behind are for me**, then still I move forward with total resolve that they **will catch up to me, eventually**.

ENMITY

*Be sober, be **vigilant**; because your adversary the devil, as a roaring lion, walketh about, seeking whom he may devour:* (I Peter 5:8)

God's revelation…

Hearing this scripture read conjures up the adversary as the devil himself or other people counted as enemies. Too often overlooked, however, is an enemy, an entity, which is ever present with us. It continuously stands actively against God's righteousness within us. Though Satan is a formidable enemy against whom we should be prepared at all times to battle, he is not omnipresent. He cannot be in all places at all times. On the other hand, always with us at the forefront of all our struggles, is an adversary which continually wars against God's Spirit in us. Certainly, at any mention of "adversary", this enemy should come to mind for us to stand against daily—sober and alert.

For 'the flesh' lusteth against the Spirit, and the Spirit against the flesh: and these are contrary the one to the other: so that ye cannot do the things that ye would **Galatians 5:17**…hence an adversary

*Because the 'carnal mind' is enmity against **God**: for it is not subject to the law of **God**, neither indeed can be.* (Romans 8:7) *God is a Spirit: and they that worship Him must worship Him in Spirit and in Truth.* (**John 4:24**)

*But every man is tempted, when he is **drawn** away of his 'own lust', and enticed.* (**James 1:14**)

Against this—my flesh—which is enmity to my God, I resolve to be sober and to be vigilant. Determined, I contend in the truth that "I am a wretch, indeed, without God. Apart from Him, there is no good thing going on in this flesh." He is **the only Good**. His Glory is my purpose and my determination. "Bought with a price, I am not my own." Therefore, I dare not attach or remain attached to anything that is not like Him.

Desiring to expose our hearts, God defines potentially adversarial operations of our Christian walk which gravely limit His call to Kingdom Building. We should be ever poised against these operating in our lives.

He says, to the **Carnal Christian**

The flesh still drives too many things and My Spirit is oppressed. The condition of your physical, mental, and psychological state drive how you treat others. Shamefully, your environment is allowed to dictate your physical and mental responses. Your misguided understanding causes you to mistake the liberty I've given you as an allowance to continue to indulge the activities of the world. You continue to pursue alcohol to settle your mind, partying and joining in the operations of the flesh to prove that you are not judgmental, shacking because you don't want to be alone, and oh, fornication, adultery, abuse, and filthy language. Not only do you act like but you look like and dress like the world, over-exposing my temple, piercing and painting it excessively. You put forth much effort trying to enhance what I have already made beautiful and changing my design. You desire a relationship with the spirit of neither sacrifice nor self-discipline. Humility is not a thing of beauty to you. You are with Me on Sunday mornings and no more. Functioning in your own strength to 'manipulate' the results you desire and to 'stay safe' from any pain and suffering, politics are the rule of your day.

Your foundation and your salvation are in question. You have traded the Truth for a lie and supported the atrocity that there are other ways to Me besides My Son. At peace with the world and its standards, your fear is of man and your reverence is to man. You are not separated. You are not set apart. There is little peculiar about you. You stand for little and fall for much. '**Nil is your witness**!

He says, to the **Textbook Christian**

You easily take to heart and live to imitate what you read or glean from a seminar. You are great at transitioning into practice both written and spoken concepts. Nevertheless, I have this against you (*Rev. 2:4*). Your spiritual maturity is limited. Appearances overshadow the Truth that your spirit man remains full of things not yet covered by what you have read or heard. Soft-spoken and sweet is your demeanor. A great teacher and leader are you. Both your demeanor and public activity project maturity. Yes, you pray diligently, you pray often, your prayers reach heaven. However, your heart remains unpurged, full of stones. Your heart, unforgiving and judgmental, is full of envy, strife, prejudice, and so on.

Diligently pursuing knowledge, you can recite My Word like the back of your hand. Also in your repertoire are self-helps, Oprah's favorites, Psychology 101, Timeout Behavior Management, and even resources aligned with witchcraft and sorcery. So busy gathering and soaking up man's input/interpretation on things—how to live, how to view Me, how to deal with your depression, how to raise your children, how to get that promotion, how to make money, etc.—that you failed to consult Me. 'God, what is your position on this? What would You have me to do?' Oh! What peace you often forfeit and what needless pains you bear, and impinge on others. All because you do not bring EVERYTHING to Me in prayer (Proverbs 3:5). You have traded my power to deliver and to transform your situation. I'm useful for 'information' in your life not 'authorship' of your life.

You are diligent, available, and busy learning of and mimicking Me. Yet, limited is your commitment to boldly follow Me. Limited by what people think, how it may appear in the physical realm, and what you've given Me rights to. **You do not believe me completely thus you quench My Spirit**.

The many works that I would do here are hampered by your unbelief. Yeah, you follow Me. You engage conversations of me. You serve in homage to Me. Yet, you keep trading My 'Supernatural' for the 'natural' thus relegating yourself to that which is in your limited grasp and man's limited ability. I have miracles available for you. Above your circumstances, dare to believe Me. Dare to look to Me. Dare to try Me. Dare to be radical for Me.

He says, to the **Compromised Christian**

Great is your desire to be true to Me, but I have this against you. You want to believe that there's innately something inside everyone that desires to do good and that you can somehow convict them into doing the right things. As a result, you can easily miss the enemy in

the midst of a matter. In grave error, when you spot the enemy, you think that you can be righteous with him and he'll be righteous back. So, you let him sit at your table, drive your car, sleep in your house and use your bed. You give Satan's advocates space in your life. That should NEVER be. You defer dealing with spiritual matters when the advocates are present by putting Me off, delaying Me, even ignoring me.

In the workplace, some of you hide even eliminate your Bibles and are careful not to mention Me. You sit idle as gossip, lies, favoritism, prejudice, bias, even racism, permeate the atmosphere. Making excuses that it is not your business or right to address it rather than looking to Me for the alternatives, the way of escape, or direction on how to stand against it. Shamefully, you agree with and are even guilty of some. You don't want to offend anyone, though all the while I'm offended. You think 'Now is not the right time' and 'I'll let it go this time and deal with it later'. Don't you know that this is a spiritual, not flesh-n-blood matter? It is about the enemies—the flesh and Satan—at work against your God. You have to stop looking at the flesh-n-blood of a matter and look intentionally for the spirit behind the matter. **Your contaminated witness grieves My Spirit**.

These adversarial operations of the flesh result in clouded, contaminated, filthy, muddied, polluted witness.

Come out from among them, My Children! Touch not the unclean thing!

To live is Christ. Anything less is dead.

Per God's direction, close your eyes for a moment and allow Him to paint a picture. "Peering down on the earth from My heavenly throne, I look into a crowd of people and you are in the midst. How do I know that you belong to Me? Choose carefully your answer. I see not only your physical state. I see your heart." says the Lord.

Paul says of it this way, "I press toward the mark…" In this he is saying, I [literally] press and war against this, my flesh, and everything in it that is unlike My God to achieve the victory that is promised. As my living is the greatest testimony to the "so great a cloud of witnesses", may I live by the legacy and truth of those that have gone on and impress Truth on those needing a witness now and those to come.

…And I call this flesh to die, in the name of Jesus. Die, flesh! Die!

In **John 12:24**, Jesus reminds us: "Verily, verily, I say unto you, Except a corn of wheat fall into the ground and die, it abideth alone: but if it dies, it bringeth forth much fruit."

When we finally get to that point of **Isaiah 6:1-5** where-in our hearts we are able to see the purity of God as measured against our filthiness and wretchedness then and only then will things begin to change. When we begin to submit to the death of this flesh, then will chains begin to fall away, yokes be broken; internal renewal and purification begin, and true Christ-likeness pursue us.

It's about being sold out and having your mind made up to "Go with Jesus, all-the-way!"

I pray… "Lord, Arrest this, my flesh. Cause everything that has quickened itself in this flesh and is against You, My God, to die. Also, Father, quicken all that lay dormant in me that is of Your will, that is like You, and that is of Your heart and my usefulness to You. May those dry bones be quickened and made alive by the power of Your Holy Spirit in Me. I claim it according to Your precious promise. *Then will I sprinkle clean water upon you, and ye shall be clean: from all your filthiness, and from all your idols, will I cleanse you. A new heart also will I give you, and a new spirit will I put within you: and I will take away the stony heart out of your flesh, and I will give you a heart of flesh.* (Ezekiel 36:25, 26) See also Ezekiel 36:23-31; 20:43; 6:9; Isaiah 6:1, 5; Job 5, 6]. By Your Spirit, cause me to walk in Your statutes and to keep Your ways."

I conclude my stand against this enmity in the words of the anointed, God appointed songwriter and singer, Mr. Tye Tribett; as he spoke it to his flesh…

_Nothing good came out of you and me
_That's why it's so easy for me to choose
_There's only one thing left for me to do
_And that's die to you…
POWERFUL!

NO REMEMBRANCE

I awoke twice one morning to the firm whisper, "No Remembrance!" Knowing then that God must have something in this for me to ponder, I jumped up and grabbed my bible along with Strong's Exhaustive Concordance intent on simply researching the word remember and building from there. However, I felt pressed by Holy Spirit to look for the exact words 'no remembrance', nothing more, nothing less.

So, I did and found this.

Ecclesiastes 1:11; 2:16...*There is no remembrance of former things: neither shall there be any remembrance of things that are to come with those that shall come after. ...For there is no remembrance of the wise more than of the fool forever; seeing that which now is in the days to come shall all be forgotten; And how dieth the wise man? As the fool.*

Holy Spirit released this for our edification as Christians. We have a great need to get this thing righteous and stop behaving like the authority and power is ours to control things. Even if we do manage to control some things and affect some outcomes in this life, we err believing our impact will last forever. Yet, the reality is that efforts born of the might of men are finite and futile.

All will meet death, cease to exist on this earth, one day, and our deeds, good or bad, will cease with us. All that has been accomplished and all that has been accumulated will be left to others. No longer remembered as attached to our names, things will begin anew with those that we leave behind.

This is ancient wisdom, spoken by men of old, but Jesus qualifies it anew: It is all vanity except **what we do for Christ** which is all that will last and be carried on after we are gone. Let us resolve to leave a legacy of righteousness toward our God, not rebellion against Him. This is imperative for the strength, success, and security of our posterity through which our legacy lives on.

Our purpose, while we yet live on this earth, is to sanctify our God in the sight of all mankind, "to make His name great!"

V

YOU ARE THE LIGHT OF TRUTH THAT SETS MEN FREE

In the meadow, in the presence of
Your Glory is a splendor so brilliant
that all darkness is eradicated.

*Be a lamp unto my feet, LORD. Illuminate my pathway
and set my course. Reveal in me the beauty of Your character
that by its light, men may be drawn to freedom in You.*

SETTING THE STANDARD

Jesus is the Righteous standard by which all our living should be measured. All that we say, do, and think should be measured against that standard.

During one meditation, the Spirit spoke to me, "It's about 'right vs. righteousness'. It's about standing against the flesh to promote the Righteousness of God." What God meant in this matter is clear to me, but He gave me an opportunity to exercise that revelation and put it in clear perspective.

Stopping at a store and grabbing necessary items for my daughter's class project, I proceeded to the checkout and sat my things on the counter waiting to be serviced. One clerk was moving about the store returning items to shelves. The second seemed to be casually conversing with a customer and her young daughter. After waiting patiently for a while and thinking, 'Maybe they don't realize that I am standing here', I said, "Excuse me. I need some help over here." Before I could get the words out, the second clerk whose back was to me exclaimed snappily, "There are only two of us in this store. We can help only one person at a time, so you'll just have to wait until we can get to you." As I'm sure you've guessed, the flesh didn't appreciate the attitude and tried to raise a response. Suppressed from responding as desired, the flesh then tried to convince me to walk out. Mind you, it was perfectly within my 'right' to walk out. After all, the clerk was rude and in the wrong.

Glory to the Master! His Righteousness which defines all and settles EVERY matter spoke to me in that moment, "Gwen, this ain't about you. This is about Me. Stand there and don't you move. You wait whatever time it takes and then you show her My love and My kindness." In obedience, I did as commanded. When she finally serviced my checkout, I spoke with a calm that was sincere; and it felt awesome. The enemy was shut down. Above this flesh, which at its best doesn't measure up, God was glorified. It was not 'right', but 'Righteous'!

Christians, too often opinions, prejudices, and logic that represent our flesh get in the way of God having His way. **The inferior keeps exceeding the superior.** "You see?" He said to me, "It's not about what is 'right'. It's about whether it is 'Righteous'."

Just prior to the time of this revelation, God had given my pastor a mission drive for our congregation called One Focus. The challenge for members was that we sign and personally commit a decree to petition God to show us just one person He has assigned us to love into the Kingdom. God spoke to my heart during service one Sunday, "I AM your ONE FOCUS!" Leading me to reflect on the episode in the store, He brought a fuller perspective. Through scripture, God summed it up, "Seek ye first the kingdom of God and His Righteousness and all these things shall be added unto you." Jesus is God's Righteousness. He is the standard that God has called His children to fervently, diligently reach for. By it, all our needs, even our desires are secured. God has given us many 'ones' with whom we will never interface directly. They, however, are watching our lives—our walk, our talk, our expressions, our worship. Our lives are a witness through which either the anointing of Jesus will flow, unto their salvation, or God forbid, in our disobedience, the contamination of the enemy will flow to their demise.

Even greater, my witness has impact beyond my circle of direct influence, beyond the sanctuary, beyond my household. I affect my children who affect others that affect others. It affects my grandchildren who affect others that affect others. It affects my great-grandchildren who affect others that affect others. It's not about me. It's so much bigger. **The Christian legacy that I establish extends to a multitude beyond my grave.** Thus, I resolve to take on the love of Christ exemplified in **John 17** and 'for their sakes I sanctify myself'.

As the Spirit put it to me: I repeat, as I have shared in the previous section of this book, the exact words of the Master...

_"Every interface is an opportunity to impress Me (Jesus) on somebody."

_ "Those with access to the Truth have NO excuse for operating in anything other than that Truth."

In other words, those of us who are saved and now have the Spirit of God residing on the inside should let it be the rule of our days. That is our charge today and always. We must put aside our opinions, our sophistication, our education, our prejudices, our biases, our favoritism, our chauvinism, our money, our social status, our color, and our other inferior stuff with a determination of the heart to live everything we do, every place we go to the Glory of the Master.

The Spirit of God in us makes it clear that there is **a more excellent way**. Let us resolve to walk in it together. Let us pray for one another that the flesh will die and that God will have His way first in us—living temples—that it may extend into the fellowship temple.

There are individuals, both present and to come, whose lives and salvation are dependent on us getting this thing RIGHTEOUS!

TRADE NOT THE TRUTH FOR A LIE

As written in II Thessalonians 2:10-12, dire is the consequence of trading the truth for a lie.

Read **John 18 and 19**. See Jesus on that cross.

- He looked guilty to man
- He looked weak
- He looked defeated
- He was marred and accursed!
- He was covered in sin before Almighty God

How bad, how major a curse it was, how great an appearance of guilt it presented mattered not for despite His innocence, His ability, and His right to come down, Jesus stayed there and finished what He had started. Amidst ridicule and scorn, the lies His situation presented did not change the Truth. Having done all (dwelt among man and established God's legacy on this earth), Jesus stood. He stayed there until what He had come to do was finished. Our sins were fully transferred to Him and He lost fellowship with His Father, as God turned His back on Him.

So, what is the Truth? Had Jesus come down off that cross or the fact that He did not, changed nothing for Him. Still as He was, He is and He will remain.

- Kings of Kings,
- Lord of Lords,
- The Righteousness of God,
- The Son of God with a place at the right hand of the Father,
- Heir to the throne,
- Intact with His kingdom in Heaven.

However, things would have changed for us, the undeserving. There would be no hope of salvation. The Cross did not reduce Him, yet it lifted us. **Thank God for the Cross**!

BEYOND THE RAINBOW
(April, 2018)

I remember, during my pregnancy with my second child, several things God had spoken and shown me of His heart regarding her. Among the things He revealed was the theme of the rainbow. **"Beyond the Rainbow"**, He said. I excitedly began to collect Noah's ark and rainbow related keepsakes for her. It was difficult, though, finding many things with the rainbow, specifically. I remember years later sharing with a friend my frustration that there seemed to be nothing out there with a rainbow theme for me to purchase for my daughter's collection. I had located mostly Noah's ark items.

What they shared with me next floored me. That God's rainbow was now being used as a symbol of something I didn't remotely identify with was of great strain to me, considering. I was not happy with the possibility of my daughter's collections possibly reflecting this. I demanded to God that He must raise up a standard against this thievery and take back this beautiful symbol of mercy that with the current use, now isolates the rest of us. I thought on this from time-to-time but few revelations came from God in response to my demand. Suddenly in late March 2018, I watched a recording of an award show in which an individual, during an award acceptance speech, in what was clearly grave and misguided error, assigned all that she had endured at the hands of individuals that exploited her in childhood (adults responsible for her care), and what led to her current way of living as: God's "training".

After I got over the strain of it, I began to hurt for her. Someone had given her counsel that has caused her to believe a lie. I began again to pray earnestly for God to open her eyes and the many others that have been deceived this way to the truth and to expose the liars and haters of God that with evil and ill-intent exploit their hurt, claiming God as the mastermind behind their painful experiences. To note: At the moment of her statement, I heard the Spirit say "Training is not in the Bible." I checked, and sure enough, the specific word "training" does not appear in the Bible, not once. What's more, God builds (or trains) us for inward, Spiritual edification, not the physical, which the Word makes clear has a nature of desire not aligned with this.

Genesis 9:16 reads clearly, *"And the bow shall be in the cloud; and I will look upon it, that I may remember the everlasting covenant between God and every living creature of all flesh that is upon the earth.* I began to reflect again on the prior strain of this beautiful symbol being isolated to one group. God then reminded me of the scripture that we be not discouraged nor dismayed, **Our God is not mocked**. He is never caught by surprise and has in advance raised up a standard. Those secure in our truth, God implores, had better be prepared to give a reason to every man that asks of the hope [the Jesus] that is in us.

There is a foundation that is established from the beginning by God in the "creation" of man. It is firm. It is solid and has not, will not, change. However, there is a foundation being set up that has its beginning only in man and its security in the confines of the mind of man. It is unstable and constantly changing its contents. It is not firm and has no inclusion in the creation process and is not a part of its story. Nothing has merit that does not equal the spoken claim and design of the Almighty. In the beginning was the Word and that Word spoke the world and its inhabitants into existence and the same Word defined the form of man. God makes no mistakes; He does not go back on His Word and never apologizes for His Truth. This Truth is established on Christ the solid rock; all other ground (all other foundations; all other views) are sinking sand.

Yes, Genesis 9 gives promise concerning the rainbow that reflects our God's mercy and grace, yet Peter affirms what we know. The same God of mercy is too a God of justice. In His justice is the coming judgement of which we are warned throughout the Word. Peter qualifies it in *2 Peter 3:9, 10* which read:

> **9.** *The Lord is not slack concerning his promise, as some men count slackness; but is longsuffering to us-ward, not willing that any should perish, but that all should come*

*to repentance. **10.** But the day of the Lord will come as a thief in the night; in the which the heavens shall pass away with a great noise, and the elements shall melt with fervent heat, the earth also and the works that are therein shall be burned up.*

As we know, the rainbow came after the flood of waters that filled the entire earth. You see, the washing of water represents simply an outward washing away as in shifting the dirt from one place to another and presents but a physical change, so to speak....but, the fire! Yet, when something burns, there's a chemical reaction taking place; and when complete, a chemical change has occurred and something totally different comes out of it. There is a separation taking place and pure substances are being released. The filthy, the nasty, the degraded stuff is canceled by it. Peter makes clear that when the world gets to the point through so-called intellectuals, scholars, and experts, that it is relentless and unrepentant in its determination to turn God's Truth into a lie, then the fire will ensue. God says, **"That is** the remainder of the promise **'beyond the rainbow'!"**

Know, Beloved, that if the stories you are told and the rational you are presented regarding the choices you have made are all feel-good validations, it is likely that what you are hearing is a lie. Training? ... If you believe that God is the director of the evil perpetrated by others in your life, you are gravely mistaken. **God only directs the process to release and deliverance**. The rest is done at the hands of the enemy.

Speaking of the fire that will ensue, I'm reminded that God in prelude to the final destruction made clear His position in this matter. He gave a foretaste through the destruction of two wicked cities that took His mercy for granted; and with unruly behavior and mockery, rejected His Truth. He rained down on them and destroyed them by fire. He purified the land which their degradations so nastily polluted.

Such a deep rejection of His position of man 'in the image of God'—is the ultimate antichrist spirit, a planting of the enemy. When one attaches him or herself to this antichrist spirit and activity of rebellion, a stronghold of disobedience is birthed (as in the two defiant cities of Genesis) to which any other sin is able to attach itself, easily. Though calling them wicked, in general, God chose to note only one specific sin. Why? He did so the make clear that this sin did not come to exist because of the wickedness, yet those two cities of Genesis became so wicked because of it. It is the ultimate rebellion into which all other sin is easily able to exist.

Finally, I am reminded, too, of the process that preluded the rainbow. Noah was directed to receive; and God sent creatures two-by-two, male and female.

> *I take back what the devil has stolen, in the name of Jesus;*
> *and but pray that every precious heart that he has deceived*
> *be retrieved.*

IN SPIRIT AND TRUTH
(October, 2011)

My Dearest Aunt Mildred is the eldest living female member of our family. She attends a church that is a member of one of the denominations that believes and teaches Saturday as the true day of Sabbath worship and rest. From time-to-time she would attend Bible Study classes with us at Mt. Zion MBC; and in October 2011, we agreed that we would visit and fellowship with her during a Bible Study at her church. In lieu of our normal Wednesday evening study, on October 9, 2011, we attended her church, instead.

After our visit, talking with God and pondering the things presented by the speaker, I'm compelled to respond to the campaign launched by him to establish, promote, and influence the belief that any day of worship, or any Sabbath, apart from Saturday is in error; yet I am especially compelled to respond to the disturbing implication that to worship on Sunday is analogous to those traveling on the wide road to destruction.

Let God be true and every man a liar. If it can't be qualified by His Word, it is NOT so. Study for yourself that you not be made ashamed for work you've done in vain.

I'm prepared to give unto every man a reason of the hope that is within me.

. . . . . .

Put simply, I'm satisfied that the God that I serve and Whose Truth witness I have living in me, is NOT THAT PETTY; nor rigid regarding something as insignificant and trivial as a 'day' of the week (where it concerns our worship and salvation).

The speaker began in the book of Revelation, as the end times study was supposed to be his focus, however, he immediately shifted the night's lesson to promote the position that "Sunday" worship is in error. He went from there to **Matthew 5:17** *Think not that I am come to destroy the law, or the prophets: I am not come to destroy, but to fulfill.*

He didn't much elaborate on this and quickly went to the scripture statement made by Jesus in Samaria when talking with the woman at the well. **John 4:23, 24** *But the hour cometh, and now is, when the true worshippers shall worship the Father in spirit and in truth: for the Father seeketh such to worship him. God is a Spirit: and they that worship him must worship him in spirit and in truth.* He further identified and read **John 17:17** *Sanctify them through thy truth: thy word is truth.*

Clearly, Jesus said, "Thy Word is Truth." He didn't say, 'thy law'. Last I checked and each time since, **John 1:1-2** reads: *In the beginning was the word and the word was with God and the word was God.* Long before the law was the word. That word is Jesus Christ.

The Bible Study leader then expressed, "You see, some people are content with just worshipping God in Spirit and without the truth. But the scripture makes it clear your worship must include the truth." He then referred to and quoted **Ezekiel 20:12** (*Moreover also I gave them my sabbaths, to be a sign between me and them, that they might know that I am the LORD that sanctifieth them.*) with intent to establish what that 'truth' is regarding the Sabbath. He further used the analogy of the narrow vs. broad way to reflect the difference between those who worship on Sundays vs. those who worship on Saturdays. **Matthew 7:13, 14** *Enter ye in at the strait gate: for wide is the gate, and broad is the way, that leadeth to destruction, and many there be which go in thereat: Because strait is the gate, and narrow is the way, which leadeth unto life, and few there be that find it.* This was the point of my brake, in which I knew I could not keep silence; the audacity to imply damnation belongs to people based solely on a difference in worship day is unacceptable.

From here he set to establish that Saturday is the accurate Sabbath. He noted our calendar as the means used for identifying the order of days of the week and since Sunday is first on the calendar, it is the first day of the week; and further made the claim that this is what we have been taught in school regarding the calendar. He sighted, as well, the vision of **Ezekiel 8:16** *And he brought me into the inner court of the LORD's house, and, behold, at the door of the temple of the LORD, between the porch* *and the altar, were about five and twenty men, with their backs toward the temple of the LORD, and their faces toward the east; and they worshipped the sun toward the east.* And further established his case against Sunday as valid because in pagan worship supposedly Sunday was set aside as a day to worship the sun.

In the course of his presentation, he further established that Saturday was the true Sabbath because that was the day of Jesus' resurrection. *"And how, then, did some get to Sunday? It didn't come from God, so it could only have been sewn by the enemy,"* he concluded. Amazingly, he ended his rhetoric with an invitation to acknowledge the truth and to turn from Sunday's error to Saturday's right as one would do during an invitation to leave a life of sin to receive salvation.

Last I checked (and always), the only invitation in the Bible to a confession is that we acknowledge Christ and all that He is. He is NOT a day of the week and my only access to Him is not restricted to only occur one day of the week. So, the only response I can give is this: "Let us examine God's heart in this matter, shall we?"

Jesus came to fulfill, to make complete, entire; to perfect, the law and by it, He set, He lived, He taught a standard that exceeds, is greater than, is purer than the law. It is of a truth that the law states to remember the Sabbath day and keep it holy. The Hebrew word is Shabbath, meaning a break in or an intermission. If we reflect on live plays or shows we attend, the intermission is an 'at ease' time—a time in which the audience gets to stop and absorb what they have just taken in, to relax their minds and refuel with snacks, etc.; as well, a time for those putting on the show to relax and to refresh their vocals, to change costumes, to prepare for the remaining show requirements, etc. This is the original intent of the Sabbath, a day hallowed by God and to serve as a time to stop the monotony of the week and to reflect on God's current and past goodness to His children when they were first given rest from their labors during Egyptian bondage and as a reflection of it as His day, considering He took His own rest (time to reflect on all that He had made) from creation on the seventh day.

The Word further implores us that the Sabbath was made for man and not man for the Sabbath—a day set aside for man to rest and reflect; a day consecrated not by man's rituals, but alone by God's sanctification of it through Jesus, the Lord of the Sabbath. The Word further teaches us that all things in creation were made by Jesus and for Jesus. No doubt, this includes not just the day on which the Jewish Sabbath falls, but ALL days of the week. The fact that Sunday was allegedly once set aside for 'sun' worship is thus, irrelevant and amounts to nothing but the contamination of the enemy; who is not the creator of the world nor equal to the creator of all things, including the days of the week. As matter of fact, Sunday is the day that the original—the New Testament—church came together to worship. ...and Paul, Peter, and John are all certainly in Heaven..

The Bible has taught us this fact: For everything of God, Satan has a cheap imitation, and what we have learned across the course of our studies and the things we have found out about him is that, he does not go after separate stuff; he does not create his own; but takes what God has created and attempts to contaminate it with his evil and filth. This being true, it is more likely (if Sunday was actually worship of the 'sun' day) that Sunday is indeed the true Sabbath, 'cause this is exactly what Satan would attempt to contaminate. No. I most certainly am not, by this, promoting Sunday any more than Saturday as the 'true' Sabbath day.

A study of biblical times and original days reveals them different from how we count them today. One difference of significance is that biblical days went from evening to evening, not midnight to midnight, whose lengths even changed periodically based on the cycle of the moon. **Genesis 1:5b, 8b, etc** read: *and the evening and the morning were the [#] day.*

As I noted prior, the speaker mentioned our calendar and how it is laid out as the standard for how we establish which day is the seventh day and because Sunday is the first day showing on the calendar, it is counted as the first day of the week and even indicated this as what we were taught in school. I don't know where his knowledge of the calendar came from, but I do vividly remember what I was taught about it. I learned Monday as the first day of the week and Sunday as the seventh. The understanding that I was given was that Sunday is set on the calendar in first position deliberately with the purpose and determination to identify it as the most valuable/reverenced day of the week, period.

Point of Information: Israel's calendar is based on the beginning of mankind and counts its years according to that. As well, they cycle their days and months based on the cycles of the moon. We go by the Gregorian calendar which tracks specific finite days and whose time spans are exactly the same day-by-day. Our years track from the birth of Jesus. Israel has a 354-day calendar year with 382-385 days (an extra month) every 2-3 years. While we have a consistent 365-day yearly calendar with only one day added every 4 years. Also, Israel is roughly ½ day ahead of us in days of the week. By this, we couldn't be exact in matching their Sabbath unless ours was a moving Sabbath—the day of the week we hold as Sabbath would have to change periodically for us to match exactly their Saturday. As well, the Saturday worshippers would have to adjust the time span they set for observance of that day as Sabbath to truly comply with a 'day of the week' requirement. **Simply put, the argument for any day as overriding the other as a true Sabbath is silly.**

GOD MADE EVIL? NO WAY!
(May 2019)

On the ride home, February 9, 2019, I was listening to radio commentary during which the speaker stated that 'God made evil'. This statement hit hard in my psyche and the strain of it felt like a ton of bricks had landed on me. "Not so, huh, Father?" Yet, I immediately canceled the thought. This is a confusing, hard to conceive one for me; so, I was probably not ready for the answer.

I took a step back from my question and left off asking God if it were true; but instead I simply pondered the inquisition, "**If so**, then why would You (God), being perfect and pure, choose to create something so opposing?"

As I rested for an answer, He took my mind back to *Genesis 1:2* (see all, *Genesis 1:1-4*). "*. . . and darkness was upon the face of the deep. . . .*" to which He responded in verse 3, "*let there be light: . . . .*" Then I heard Him say,

> *"In order for light to have an identity, darkness had to exist."*

Simply, as I received it in spirit, 'In order for light to have a purpose, there has to be a need for it.'

> *Let us pray one for the other, Beloved: that we actively pursue excellence in this Christian journey that the light of Christ might pierce forth—first eradicating the darkness in us, while exiting through us to expose Him to the world— that the evil darkness of the enemy might be overtaken by it and that men might see and come to desire that same cleansing and purifying power of the Son.*

Genesis 2:4 reads: *And God saw the light, that it was good: . . .* Thank God for the light! It confuses; it cancels; it overtakes darkness.

VI

YOU ARE NEW LIFE, THE UNADULTERATED WORD, THE INNOCENCE IN ME

In the meadow of Your Holiness
are 'fresh' views

Guide my Christian journey, Dear Lord. Let the legacy of Your Truth live on beyond my life span, but continue through those I leave behind.

And a Little Child Shall Lead Them…

The **LORD**
is the portion of mine
INHERITANCE
and of my cup:
thou maintainest my lot.
The lines are fallen unto me
in pleasant places;
yea, I have a goodly **[BEAUTIFUL]**
HERITAGE.
Psalm 16:5-6

Our purpose is Kingdom-building, directing lives to the cross, and ministry. The first ministry is in our families.

IMAGE

(February 2015)

Black History month, about 3 years ago, God had given the message that posed the question: "What's your perspective?" This question was getting us thinking about how we look at our history and how we let it drive us today and into the future. Do we have "right" (or might I say "righteous") perspective about this thing called our 'Black History'—the wonderful history and legacy that it is? This time, I heard God say: IMAGE…

What God gave me in those moments holds true for all Christianity. God wants to know of His Christian children, "What is your perspective?"; "What story are you telling?"; "What IMAGE are you portraying?" As children of God, it is our responsibility to tell HIS story. One evangelist, a painter, on one of his television episodes spoke of it this way: Your life is a canvas and every day you paint a bit of your history on it and at the end of your life, imagine: that canvas is put on display, 'What story does it tell?'

So far, what does your portrait reveal? God is asking of us.

Our reflection of our Christian family is analogous to that of our physical families. Early in life there are some physical traits and similarities that support the truth that we belong to our families; and as we grow and develop to increasing independence, and as we shed our 'baby fat', many more traits--not only in physical features, but even in personality—make it clear and even more unquestionable the truth of it.

I know for me: the resemblance in features and personality have become so clear that people no longer approach and ask, but now they tell me what 'family' I belong to; and when I ask how they know, they begin to point out the many obvious traits—the IMAGE of my parents and of the Alexander family—that I reflect.

…And as I thought on all this, God gave me **"IMAGE"**

God's question this year?
IMAGE…..What are you putting on display?

147

IMAGE

That IMAGE of HIStory, That IMAGE that you see
Is it reflective of Me?
A portrait of painting, who do you see?
Your IMAGE, your stature, your personality.
A reflection of you; your legacy.

To draft an IMAGE; to tell a story
Is your life's expectancy
A portrait, a canvas to paint of thee
Be careful the choice and match of colors, you see
For every stroke is a reflection of family

Live passionately
Love determinately
With Jesus, in sacrificial harmony
For beyond the grave this IMAGE lives, through your posterity
It is through them, that you (or He), the world will likewise see

When you in that coffin lay, lifelessly
What will it be of your IMAGE on display to see?
Will in Truth there be a ceremony?
Our will they tell a story that is phony?
Because your IMAGE, with Jesus does not agree

The painting on canvas, that IMAGE of thee
Does it reveal, hip hop, twerking, and rivalry;
Or addictions—drugs, alcohol, gambling—plaguing thee;
Or shacking, fornication, adultery;
Or does it showcase the Savior's imagery?

There it is in *Colossians Chapter 3*
A call to shed the baby fat, you see
That you heed the call to live righteously
That it be God who governs thee
To reveal the blood of Jesus in maturity

Not by that which is viewed physically
Not by whether bond nor free
But that Christ is in thee
That by His blood you've been made free
And there on that canvas lay a portrait of Christianity.

In Truth, to write your history
Is to display but His IMAGE; the world to see
Does that IMAGE reveal you of this family;
As part of HIS Story;
Or does your portrait feature that other family?

That IMAGE of HIS-story, That IMAGE that you see
Is it a Reflection of Me? says He
Is in the cross of the Savior your glory?
Only one question can there be:
Does your IMAGE but promote and celebrate My legacy?

God is speaking to us a history that He has defined,
if we would but listen and submit to it.

A legacy, a HIS-story, an **IMAGE** worth putting on display.

"HIS BEAUTIFUL CREATION"
Audriana Harris Mason (age 22), 2011

Such a young girl
With wounds so deep
Scarred by her past
And
The secrets she keeps.
Really not knowing
What love is *supposed to be.*

Haunted by the past
Her innocence gone,
Can't take it
No more!
Who could she have told?
No one to Believe her
As her stories unfold.

She took her pain
And hid it real deep
Giving up on life
and
All its meaning.
Never trusting *anyone,*
Never believing.

Just when the end
Seemed the better choice,
She felt His presence in her heart.
Dear God.
That was her voice.
Help me Father
I NEED YOU!!

He answers.
"Yes, My child.
I can hear you.
I know your pain.
I have been here all along
Watching over and Keeping you
Through the toughest storm.

Just give Me your pain,
I will make you all better.
Trust and believe
I will take care of the past.
The present, you live it.
The future's fulfilled,
I don't make mistakes with my creations.

Love yourself child because I said so.
Your smile is amazing;
Your passion so strong.
Be bold, Keep faith, Pray daily.
You are My child
Truly blessed
My beautiful creation."

"THAT'S PREPOSTEROUS"
Wayman McLaughlin III (age 18), 2010

Preposterous is the idea that we are limited in capacity to achieve.
Rather, we are limited in our ability to believe.

Preposterous means contrary to common sense;
While also meaning, it's not common to make cents.

The proposition of an Idea can leave you to hear
An infuriated "That's preposterous" in your ear.

Who's to say what's ridiculous and what is acceptable?
Some people think only with cash, checks, and decimals.

To appreciate my knowledge, you must look much deeper.
Creativity is a student who needs a thorough teacher.

Emotional emphasis on ingenious ideas is a present.
The beautiful cerebral skies open up like the heavens.

Was it preposterous to say one day that man would fly?
Because if so, reiterate to the men up in the sky.

Preposterous is a word that is frequently heard.
Anything different or new is completely absurd.

Expand your mind and stare deep in the stars.
The same thing the inventors did before the roads had cars.

Preposterous in someone's eyes is genius to me.
Over criticizing the creativity of others is a disease.

Preposterous is poison down the throat of imagination
That can only be cured through the medicine of creation.

To all be similar or the same would be a shame.
I would rather be preposterous so you remember my name.

Preposterous, a word meaning *"absurd, or contrary to common sense"*, is very controversial to me. Although this word was not often used by my family, it was used quite frequently in my community. Usually the term preposterous is heard being hurled towards a creative idea that someone has or a proposal of something different. My earliest recollection of the word was phrased "That's preposterous!" in response to a statement that I made when I was little about making an underwater car. Even at a young age, I knew it meant that my idea was unrealistic, dumb, and utterly ridiculous. Needless to say, thereafter, I have not cared for the word nor used it much in written or oral dialogue.

Preposterous has always been an extremely iffy, on the fence word for me. Mainly because I ponder, "Who's the judge of a great idea?" Envy, more often than not, leads one to demean another's new, up and coming idea. As a young child, I felt restricted as if creativity was prohibited. My point, preposterous is just the opinion of some people who haven't opened their eyes to all the possibilities. Feeling like I could get much more creative with the word through poetic prose, I elected to compose a poem. The way I see it, most inventions and great accomplishments have been achieved by people who were told that their ideas were preposterous. Imagination is an incredible thing and should not be hindered by anybody or any word. To accomplish great things, one must have the courage not only to act on limited knowledge but to believe in the possibilities despite insufficient evidence.

I wanted to take you on a journey different from that which you have come to expect, expand your mind, broaden your scope by composing a poem relevant to the assignment. The poem allowed me to creatively display my passion for metaphor, rhyme, and rhythm. Through this medium, I was better able to express the multifaceted aspects of my thoughts, imaginings, if you will, regarding the subject. A connection with my audience was desired; however, more than that I wanted you to allegorically understand my perception of the word, "Preposterous". The dynamics of gaining knowledge and expressing thought vary broadly between individuals. Personally, rhythm and rhyme are easier than long MLS formatted essays. It supports my ability to dig deeper and express my thoughts more profoundly with fewer words.

Peer perspective may be that it is preposterous to provide a thorough definition and perspective of one word through poetry. For someone to look for quantity over quality of written material is preposterous. To stretch this to a 1,000 word essay is an example, personification of exactly what I was trying to communicate in the earlier writing. Exactly why, I wanted to do things differently. To accomplish great things, one must have the courage not only to act on limited knowledge but to believe in the possibilities despite insufficient evidence.

BELIEVING IS SEEING
Juaquoya McLaughlin (age 15), 2009

I CAN NOT BELIEVE …
JUST BECAUSE MY SKIN IS BLACK
THAT IS ALL YOU SEE
THE COLOR OF ME
A CHILD OF THE MAN
DON'T YOU UNDERSTAND
OPEN YOUR EYES AND SEE
THERE IS MORE TO ME

I CAN NOT BELIEVE …
YOU JUDGE AND FIND ME WANTING
BUT KNOW WHAT YOU THINK
(WITH ME) DOES NOT LINK
I'VE BEEN GIVEN MUCH
AND REPRESENT SUCH
OPEN YOUR EYES AND SEE
ALL THE PARTS OF ME

I CAN NOT BELIEVE …
PREJUDICE CLOUDS YOUR VISION
THO WE ARE THE SAME
ONE TRUE GOD WE CLAIM
AS ONE YOU AND ME
BY DEITY
OPEN YOUR EYES AND SEE
I HAVE BEEN SET FREE

NO LONGER ENSLAVED
THE BACKGROUND YOUR STAGE
A BORN LEADER I RISE
THE STANDOUT IN A CROWD

LIBERATING A NATION
RESPECTING GOD'S CREATION
DARING TO FLEE
FROM PREJUDICES

BELIEVING IS SEEING ...
BELIEVING IS FREEING...

GOD IS GRACE
Yendami Alexander (age 17), 2013

God
Is
My strength.
When I fall,
He lifts me up and
When I am lost, he finds me
He brings peace, holds on to me, and doesn't let
Me go, even though, I have wronged. He loves me in spite
Provides for me, cares for me, has mercy on
Me, lets me live, breathe, walk and
Dwell upon this earth
And To me
That is
His
Grace

TRUST IN THE LORD
Charlie Davidson (age 16), 2013

All I have seen teaches me to trust the creator for all I have not seen.
Ralph Emerson

Trust in the Lord.
You cannot depend on your mind
…It is limited

You must let faith guide
…It goes beyond vision and thought.

Know that God works in all things
…Forever keeping His hand on you.

Alone, we are not strong
… God's help gives us power to endure.

In the dark times, when you are weary
…Our awesome God sheds light and gives you strength.

Not your judgment
…He will lead you without fail.

Trust in the Lord.

ADVANTAGE
Gnywe Smith (age 11), 2011

I'm extra tall,
Big feet and all.
My momma says,
I've got it all.

I'll take it to the court,
Gonna play them sports.
But my momma says,
That's not my last resort.

Academics,
Ain't no gimmick.
My momma says,
"In it to win it."

My life's not man's to bandage.
I give it to God to manage.
"Now," Momma says,
"You got the advantage!"

I THANK THE WONDERFUL GOD WHO CREATED ME!

Nigel Alexander (age 13), 2013

I thank the wonderful God who created me,
Who has done so many things to make my life great,
Who has provided me with wonderful parents
And family that loves me.
Without Him where would I be?

I thank the Almighty God who created me,
Who loved the world and gave his son, the begotten one.
Whosoever believes in Him shall not perish
But have everlasting life.
Now I have life and an opportunity to make something of myself.
I refuse to waste that opportunity because that's not what I'm about.

I thank the magnificent God who made me,
Who created me unique;
I came with special features, I stand out, His technique.
I am defined by Song of Solomon 4:7
My Lord proclaimed, "I am altogether beautiful… there is no flaw in me."
This means God made me exactly how he wanted me to be.

I'm not perfect but I try… my best to pursue perfection.
Therefore I will not give up until I have become the best me I can be!
I will set the bar for the level of awesomeness.
I thank God, the wonderful God who created me, Me!

BEAUTY IS
Shekinah McLaughlin (age 8), 2009
(What's on the Inside)

I am blessed to be
The richest girl on E (earth)
Because God is within me.
That makes me a beauty.

Like a butterfly
Comes out of a cocoon,
Good friends bring out the best in me
Like the beautiful smiling (crescent) moon.

Like holiday sweets
From my grandma's stove,
Nice teachers warm my heart
Like the summer sun that glows.

Because my heart is beautiful
Singing songs of glory give me satisfaction
I have peace inside of me
And God controls my actions.

GOD'S UNFAILING LOVE
Neziah Smith (age 12), 2013

God's Unfailing Love
Is what my heart is full of
It never sways
Is the same all-the-day

Like rain, it showers down
No better grace I've found
Like a dove
Pure light from above

Love that fills all empty holes
That Cleanses body and soul
Was the blood of Jesus shed
Our covering set

By His everlasting covenant unveiled
His love never fails

WHO GOD IS
Zneyah McLaughlin (age 9), 2012

Listen up!

I am trying to tell you
Who God is.

He is the alpha and omega,
The Creator,
Prince of Peace,
Redeemer and Friend.

God is the one who made you.
God is the one who saves you.
You should love Him
Because he first loved you.

What does it mean?
Actually, a lot of things.

He loves you so much.
He died on the cross.
He rose from the dead
To save you from sin.

God is Good.
He's always there.
He takes care of you and me.
He makes miracles happen.

We need to pray and thank Him
But, of this I am sure…

Love and Believe Him, you must

GOD IS

Alexandria Davidson (age 6), 2011

God is the ground that we walk on
He is the air that we breathe
This is God, Our Father, and what he means to me.

SALUTATION

To My Merciful, Provisional God be the Glory.

Hallelujah! The presence of the Lord is here! I can feel it in the atmosphere for I have breathed Him in and now release Him out. Each cycle of breath begins with an inhale then concludes with an exhale. May the power of our exhale arrest the hearts of many—through our conversation, our worship, our praise, our prayer, our ministry, our dance. In every aspect of the way we live may we release Jesus. He 'alone' is worthy.

> Go in Peace.
>> Go in Grace.
>>> Go in Love.

Simply, 'Go in Jesus' for He is all these things.

... Jesus is **our Peace** offering. He is that sacrificial offering availing peace between us and God. No matter our circumstance, therein rests our calm contentment. Though storms may rage round about us, that line upward between us and God remains undisturbed. Through it, regulating our minds and hearts, He settles us.

... Jesus is Truly **the Grace** of God made present on this earth by none other than the hand of Almighty God. He is mercy. God's mercy awes me for by it my deserved punishment is by-passed. He is Grace. God's grace blows my mind for by it I'm freely given honor and blessings I could never hope to earn. Where sin abounds, Grace abounds more. In excess of our sin, in excess of our need for salvation, Jesus abounded.

... Jesus is **the Love** of God expressed in the flesh. Without condition, He came from His kingdom on high—from a position of provider to a position of need— to save my damnable soul. All He asks in return is that I allow Him to live in me and shine that same love through my heart. Unwavering, He does it all. The only requirement is that I let Him.

That, I exhale!

Thus saith the Lord God unto these bones; Behold, I will cause breath to enter into you, and ye shall live: …And I will lay sinews upon you, and will bring up flesh upon you, and cover you with skin, and put breath in you, and ye shall live; and ye shall know that I am the Lord. …So I prophesied as He commanded me, and the breath came into them, and they lived, and stood up upon their feet, **an exceeding great army**.

Ezekiel 37:5, 6, 10

ACCOLADES

To my dear sister, Jacqueline A. McLaughlin, my editor:
I appreciate your time and effort reviewing this manuscript. I am so grateful to God for your intensity and candidness sharing your input and pressing me to insure clarity and effectiveness of my writings. Thanks for standing firmly on principles of grammar to drive agreement in written expression. Your effort was instrumental toward completing a document of highest quality. I love you.

To my Broadmoor Baptist Church Family:
I am so grateful to God for making the assignment and sending me to you. Thanks for adopting me and nurturing me during my Shreveport, LA stay. Your expressions of love and encouragement have been of great value to me. Thank you for the forum to share many of these writings with you. Herb, I am most grateful for your insight and sensitivity to the Spirit to allow the platform. A multitude of blessings and continued prosperity to each of you.

To my Mt. Airy Baptist Church Family:
I bless God continually for you. For over 18 ½ years you nurtured me. It is with you that the power and presence of the Almighty was impressed on me in a most profound way. Much of my maturing, revelations, and enlightenment are attributable to my experiences with you. A more excellent living God impressed on me through you. May the outpouring and power of the Spirit remain in you, and may you stand a beacon light of the Boutte, LA community, always.

To my Mt. Zion Missionary Baptist Church Family:
You raised me. Your blood is in my veins. I'm grateful for you, my Christian and blood family. You were the center of activities that drove my upbringing and have established the foundation of my belief. There is indeed no place like home. I'm so glad that God chose small, hick Sontag, MS for me. You are indeed the source of the strength that has enabled me to stand through many adversities and failures. What God has imparted through you is the reason that I am still standing.

To my New Covenant Christian Fellowship Church Family:

You have taken up the gavel, allowing me to use my talents as you faithfully call on me for ministry opportunities. You keep me on my toes, sharpening and refining my knowledge in order to deliver a word to a diligent people, hungry for it. Thanks, Pastor Noel. You are a man who truly hears from God. Your insight to use me to teach a singles class at NCCFC is forcing the unfolding of another book that God has placed in me. I am so grateful for the opportunity to be used by God through you.

REFERENCES

The New Pilgrim Bible (KJV Student Edition), King James Version Bible, Copyright, Oxford University Press, 2003

The New Strong's Exhaustive Concordance of the Bible, Copyright, Thomas Nelson Publishers, 1990

The World Book Encyclopedia, Copyright World Book, Inc., 1985; A-Volume 1, page 154; N*O-Volume 14, page 679; Q*R-Volume 16, pages 242-3

University of Michigan KJV Bible – Browse; http://quod.lib.umich.edu/k/kjv/browse.html

Note Regarding Rainbow Colored, Star-shaped Logo (on back cover, to the left, just below the author's bio):

This logo was originally impressed on me by the Holy Spirit. Five years later, God used my youngest daughter, Neziah, to envision its final design. This logo represents the different colors of the bible shaping a cross.

- *At the center of this cross is the sun representing the glory of God (which is Jesus, himself)*
- *with orange outlining it to represent the burning/purging/purifying power of the Son.*
- *Blue is (water) the Holy Spirit; our source of access, fellowship, and renewal in righteousness and truth*
- *Green is prosperity (especially spiritual, but monetary, as well);*
- *Red is victory (through the blood of Christ by which we bypass damnation);*
- *Purple is royalty into which we have been adopted as sons of God;*
- *White is cleansing and return to innocence as acquired through Jesus, our propitiation.*

NOTES

NOTES

NOTES